Acronyms
Building
Character

The ABCs of Life

by

Bruce Brummond

Acronyms Building Character: The ABCs of Life, Bruce Brummond

Library of Congress Cataloging-in-Publication Data

Brummond, Bruce

Library of Congress Control Number: 2005909120

ISBN-10: 0-9788486-0-8
ISBN-13: 978-0-9788486-0-6

Cover photos of Bruce Brummond and Skipper at Stadium High School provided by StrodeMcGowan Photography, Tacoma, Washington

Printed in the United States of America

Introduction

Acronyms Building Character
The ABCs of Life

This book contains hundreds of unique acronyms to help you get along with yourself and those around you. If you are currently on the planet and have a pulse, this entertaining approach to character building will be invaluable to you, your family, friends, and associates.

TRY
To
Respect
Yourself

SMILE
Sure
Makes
It
Lots
Easier

WORK
We
Only
Respect
Kindness

FUN
Forget
Unnecessary
Nonsense

SUCCESS
Seek
Understanding
Carefully;
Character
Eventually
Sows
Satisfaction

NICE
Never
Insult
Compliment
Everyone

LIE
Losers
Intentionally
Exaggerate

IDEA
Inspiration
Deserves
Everyone's
Attention

BOSS
Big
On
Securing
Success

GOSSIP
Guarded
Old
Secrets
Sensationalized
In
Public

HUMOR
Help
Undo
My
Ordinary
Response

LAUGH
Levity
Always
Underscores
Good
Habits

Contents

Foreword

"Bruce is a great storyteller, and the uniqueness of his acronyms enables the reader to recall significant words and ideas. You'll thoroughly enjoy this book, as he's included many real-life examples that anyone can empathize with. I've known Bruce for 40 years, and everything he does is done with passion, enthusiasm and common sense.

I highly recommend it!"

—Bob Moawad, Edge Learning Institute

Preface

Would you like to get along with yourself and those around you better? Would you like to know if you're "there" when and if you get "there?" Would you like an incredible amount of **help** in contemplating your response to these questions?

Would you like to nourish your self-**love** and **enable** yourself to develop more meaningful relationships? Would you like to be introduced to a myriad of original insights and methods to assist you in achieving a more fulfilling life? Would you like to discover how your **life** can mean Love Is For Everyone?

This book is a compilation of **true** stories (some names are changed), anecdotes, quotes, lighthearted moments, lessons, and questions entwined amidst hundreds of words that are indelibly defined by their acronyms to help you embrace your life and challenge you to experience a more successful existence. This adventure will thoroughly engage your thought processes, and the acronyms will provide a methodology to help you acknowledge your discoveries.

Make this document your template for guiding your existence. Take notes between the lines, in the margins; highlight, circle, underline, reread the chapters until you understand their implications. Develop a systematic approach for memorizing the acronyms to help you remember and share the concepts.

Alter the acronyms to fit your exact situations and **needs**. Allow this to be a springboard to developing your own unique insights and **ideas** to help you in your quest for happiness. Please read the

HELP
Hurry
Everyone
Loves
Progress

LOVE
Light's
On
Very
Empowering

ENABLE
Everybody
Needs
A
Big
Lift
Eventually

LIFE
Love
Is
For
Everyone

TRUE
To
Rely
Upon
Everything

NEEDS
Notice
Everyone's
Esteem
Develop
Successfully

IDEA
Inspiration
Deserves
Everyone's
Attention

HOPE
Harnessing
Optimism
Produces
Empowerment

chapters in numerical order; discover the treasures throughout the book as your reward for caring about yourself.

No simple solutions, explanations, catch phrases, or applicable acronyms can totally quantify the challenges in our lives in a neat and orderly fashion. We humans are colossal, complicated collections of experiences that develop and cast our character in a myriad of mysterious ways.

I sincerely **hope** the introspective journey you are taking through these pages will help you become the person you want to live with for the rest of your life.

CHAPTER 1

CHANGE

<u>C</u>ertain <u>H</u>abits <u>A</u>lways <u>N</u>egatively <u>G</u>round <u>E</u>veryone

Do you think it might be time to have a checkup from the neck up with the person who is currently wearing your clothes? Would you agree that we spend most of our lives trying to determine what to change in our everyday existence? Is there anything you would like to change in your life that would help you balance your **purpose**, **pleasure**, and **peace** of mind?

One absolute in our lives is that change is constant whether we like it or not. Our self-satisfaction is usually in direct correlation to our ability to **adapt** to change. We need to remember that the only way to achieve permanent change is to be willing to change permanently.

Consider that a fifty year old has spent half a million hours developing **habits**. If some of these habits aren't precisely what they should be, altering them can be a daunting task. It can be difficult to accept that our first goal must be a desire to change.

Let's examine the correlation between **desire** and **goals**. If you were asked a simple question such as, "Can you run a marathon, all 26.2 miles, six months from now?" you would probably say something like, "Not me . . . I could never do that! As a matter of **fact**, I think driving that far is tough enough!"

What if I mentioned to you, "I'd like to tell you about a project an extremely wealthy friend of mine is developing? This fellow is very interested

PURPOSE
Producing
Ultimate
Rewards
Produces
Our
Self-respect
Effectively

PLEASURE
Pain
Leaves
Eventually
And
Serenity
Unfolds
Refreshing
Everyone

PEACE
Practicing
Effective
Attitudes
Calms
Everyone

ADAPT
Always
Developing
Attitudes
Providing
Trust

HABITS
Harmful
Actions
Blindly
Injuring
Thoughts'n
Success

DESIRE
Does
Everyone
Strive
In
Reaching
Excellence

GOALS
Goodness
Only
Awaits
Labor—
Start

FACT
Finding
Actual
Circumstances
True

in studying the health benefits people receive from long-distance running. He will be hiring people to train and run a marathon in under five hours. Are you interested?"

Oh, you say, you are not interested. Well, maybe I should mention that this rich friend lives near Seattle, Washington, and helped start a software company that has placed him at the very top of a list of the wealthiest people in the world. Still not interested?

Apparently I neglected to mention the benefits package. He will provide you with all the necessities for the workouts—trainers, massage therapists, shoes, clothing, lodging, meals, transportation, etc., plus give you a wage commensurate with your current salary. Not interested?

Oh, I neglected to mention that he will pay all expenses for your friends and **family** to visit you at your training site as often as they like during your workout time. Not interested?

I forgot to mention that your work week will average about two hours per day on the island of Maui, Hawaii, or any place else in the world you select. Still not interested?

What if I mentioned that my rich friend will hand you a check for ten million dollars as you cross the finish line of the marathon? Now are you interested? Are you beginning to have a more thorough understanding of the correlation between your desires and your goals?

The first requirement to effect change is to develop a **desire** to change. That's up to you. The first step is your **acceptance** of your **need** for change. This is much easier if you can establish your **vision** to realize the value in your pursuits. Bingo! Life becomes much more challenging and rewarding; **boredom** is over.

I am very proud to say that I have completed four marathons. The training began when I was forty-five years old. A hereditary back disease has put my running on hold for a while. I'm not training again . . . **yet**.

By far the toughest part of training for marathons is that first step. I'm talking about that first step to get out of bed to prepare to go out the door to run. Let's **hope** that you now **want** to take that first step in your life to change the **habits** that negatively ground you and impede your **progress** toward reaching your desired level of **success**.

Analyzing and recognizing the habits we hope to change is the first huge step toward actual change. Remember, if you are going to train for the marathon of a fulfilling and **happy** life, you have to accept the fact that your feet need to leave that nice cozy, comfy bed.

William James (1842–1910), an American psychologist, said, "The greatest discovery of my generation is that a human being can alter his life by altering his attitudes of mind."

Let's take a look at some aspects of our lives to see what we might change to **help** us attain our purpose, pleasure, and peace of mind. One complicated, threatening thread that entwines most of our societies is summed up in one word: *negativism*.

Have you considered that you might be allergic to negativism? I am! After serving as a high-school choir director and a district administrator for four decades, I'm certain of that fact. I have concluded

FAMILY
Friends
Always
Manage
Inspirational
Love
Ya know

DESIRE
Does
Everyone
Strive
In
Reaching
Excellence

ACCEPTANCE
All
Circumstances
Can
Eventually
Produce
Truth
And
Negate
Certain
Excuses

NEED
Notice
Everyone's
Esteem
Develop

VISION
Very
Intense
Statement
Indicating
Objectives
Necessary

BOREDOM
Bring
On
Relationships
Ending
Doldrums
Over
Me

YET
Yes
Eventually'n
Time

HOPE
Harnessing
Optimism
Produces
Empowerment

WANT
Wishes
Always
Need
Time

that habits of **negative** thought patterns and speech patterns are the basis for most of our personal unhappiness and the conflicts we create.

This fact certainly isn't a **secret**; however, many people disagree with it. It's interesting that they are usually the people who should be changing their negative thought and behavior patterns!

A few years ago, we invited a person to make a presentation to the choirs at our school. We discovered this individual's presentations included a tremendous amount of negativity. I listened to the same presentation during five classes in a row. The following day, I found myself apologizing to the students for the negativity that I had been using myself . . . duh!

This calamity of character is termed "garbage in, garbage out." After I apologized to the students, I attempted to revert back to my usual attempts of "goodness in, goodness out." It was very difficult; however, it was a terrific learning experience for all of us to be reminded of the importance of the role models we need to select if we wish to be **positive** individuals.

One simple way to avoid being negative is to avoid using words that contain apostrophe *Ts*. You know—words like shouldn't, couldn't, wouldn't, can't, don't, won't, etc. As an example, imagine that within the next five minutes while you are reading this, a news team will show up at your location to record your thoughts about this book for a segment that will air, unedited, on your local television news channel tomorrow night. They will ask you some very specific questions, and you probably won't have a clue what the correct answer should be. Don't get nervous; they won't be aware that you are unprepared to speak any way but incoherently. You know you aren't a good speaker under pressure; let's hope you won't get a horrendous case of butterflies. But don't worry, the newscast will be seen by only about one million people. Hopefully, it won't hit the national news, so don't fret about being a blithering **idiot** in front of about half a billion people. Are you shaking? I am!

Did you pay any attention to the words with the apostrophe *T*s? Or did you simply notice the words following them? What if you read the same basic information disseminated this way: A small group of really nice people will be dropping by your place to get your personal feelings about the book you are currently reading. I know you will really like them. They are very pleasant, and they'll have you laughing a whole bunch. Remember they are only interested in your personal feelings about this book; whatever you say will be sensational. Simply speak to them as you would to any group of friends you have invited to your place. Imagine the camera is just one very close friend of yours who will eventually be viewing this **fun** discussion between some very terrific people.

Does this example help you understand the impact of negative statements on your level of **confidence**? Would you agree that the first statement had the butterflies fluttering all over your insides? Hopefully, the second example trained that same flock of cute little critters to fly in formation! Wayne Dyer, inspirational speaker and author sums up this concept very succinctly by stating, "When you change the way you look at things, the things you look at change."

HABITS
Harmful
Actions
Blindly
Injuring
Thoughts'n
Success

PROGRESS
People
Reform
Or
Garner
Refinement
Establishing
Some
Success

SUCCESS
Seek
Understanding
Carefully
Character
Eventually
Sows
Satisfaction

HAPPY
Have
All' the
Pleasure'n
Peace
Y'want

HELP
Hurry
Everyone
Loves
Progress

NEGATIVE
Never
Enjoy
Goodness
Always
Treat
Individuals
Very
Egotistically

SECRET
Sure
Everyone
Carefully
Reserves
Elaborate
Truths

POSITIVE
Please
Offer
Sincere
Insights
To
Instill
Values
Effectively

You probably have many places in mind that you would like to visit on your future vacations. Most people have visions of several years, or a lifetime, of places to go, people to see, and things to do.

Imagine that you decided to go on a back-to-nature camping trip. You would probably prepare for the trip by talking to several people and doing extensive research. The preparation can certainly be a vacation unto itself. You are no longer **bored**; just thinking about the relaxation, fun, and adventure gives you tons of joy! Dorothy Parker (1893–1967), an American author and short-story writer, said, "The cure for boredom is curiosity; there is no cure for curiosity."

While planning this trip, you would want to discover how your hobbies and interests could be fulfilled while you remain within your budget. You would probably look forward to having lots of fun with your friends and family, and you would want to be in a situation **free** from everyday **stress**.

Let's imagine that you successfully complete all the planning and preparations. You gather your camping expedition partners and head out into the hinterlands. You pitch your tent, build a fire, organize the cooking supplies, find the water, break out your toys, do some decorating, and discuss who will be responsible for which tasks, meal times, etc.

Now imagine that it's time to explore the surrounding countryside; it's a beautiful day . . . everybody's really excited. You gather the folks you would like to take along on your adventure, grab some snacks and beverages, punch your location into your Global Positioning System, and away you **go**.

When you're done exploring and it's time to head back to camp for dinner, you simply turn on your **GPS,** and that sweet little unit will lead you right back to your camp!

What if you viewed your life as a sojourn just like that **vision** of your camping trip? What if the GPS in your life stood for "Go Places Successfully?" What if the CAMP in your life were an acronym for the ingredients in the personal happiness that you are searching for? Just as you organized your camp in the woods, would your goal be to place the elements of your life in order of their importance to you?

Suppose that the elements of the CAMP in your life are Competition, Acclaim, Money, and People. Would you agree that placing these elements in order of their importance to you would help you establish a much clearer picture of what balances your purpose, pleasure, and peace of mind?

I must confess that when I was a young, single, egotistical high-school choir director, I organized my CAMP in that order: C-A-M-P. Was I happy? Go figure! Now I place those letters in a dramatically different order. How do you order the letters in the word *CAMP* to help guide your life?

Would you agree that our definition of character is a major factor in helping us determine if we are experiencing a successful life? Denish D'Souza, an American author and speaker, sums up the concept in this manner. "Success is defined as one's ability to tell the difference between right and wrong, and to strive as best as humanly possible to do what's right. To me success and goodness are synonymous."

In simpler terms, if any type of a team were composed of individuals who possess outstanding character, would it be natural to conclude that the group would be known for its integrity and,

IDIOTS
Individual's
Debilitating
Ideas
Offends
Team

FUN
Forget
Unnecessary
Nonsense

CONFIDENCE
Changing
Our
Negative
Fears
Invites
Delightful
Experiences
Never
Considered
Easy

BORED
Bring
On
Recreation
Every
Day

FREE
Feel
Renewed
Empowerment
Everyday

STRESS
Sure
Tough
Regularly
Exercising
Self
Sacrifice

GO
Great
Opportunity

GPS
Go
Places
Successfully

VISION
Very
Intense
Statement
Indicating
Objectives
Necessary

CAMP
Competition
Acclaim
Money
People

LAUGH
Levity
Always
Underscores
Good
Habits

consequently, the organization would enjoy even more success?

Shall we look at another definition of character? Webster defines character as "[t]he complex of ethical or personal traits marking a person, group or nation." How about if we sum it up in a handful of words: "Personal qualities that determine responses?"

How might we define our success in finding our **CAMP?** Man, oh, man! That's a tough one. We would probably agree that success certainly means lots of different things to different people. Webster says to succeed is "to turn out well . . . to obtain a desired object or end." Might that mean to live a long time and make a lot of money? What do you think it means? "To turn out well," "to obtain a desired object or end"? What do you desire?

Does this poem published by Bessie Stanley in 1905 and attributed to Ralph Waldo Emerson provide a template to help us prioritize our CAMP to enable us to experience a successful life?

A Definition of Success

To **laugh** often and much:
to win the respect of intelligent people
and the affection of children;
to earn the appreciation of honest critics
and to endure the betrayal of false friends;
to appreciate beauty;
to find the best in others;
to give of one's self;
to leave the world a bit better,
whether by a healthy child, a garden patch,

or a redeemed social condition;
to have played and laughed with enthusiasm
and sung with exultation;
to know that even one life has breathed easier
because you have lived.

This beautiful poem encompasses three basic expectations for our lives. Do we want to include fun in everything that we do? Do we want to help as many people as possible, receiving self-respect in return? Finally, do we hope to live a long time, so we can reap our rewards? These happen to be the precise points that my high-school classmates and I ponder when we reminisce at our annual parties.

My high school graduating class has a reunion picnic every summer. We have a fabulous time! The downside of our party is realizing that many of our classmates aren't on this earth anymore to help us celebrate life's joys. Many years after our graduation, our parties are attended by fewer people, and the events are taking on an entirely new atmosphere. We are done competing with each other, we are finished trying to impress one another, and popularity concerns are a thing of the past. It certainly doesn't matter who has made the most money if that person isn't still alive to spend it!

These are the questions we seem to always **ask** one another: "Has your **life** been filled with **fun** and **humor**? Have you been able to affect many people in positive ways by using your **gifts** and **talents**? How has your family life been? And oh, by the way, have you been eating right and exercising on a regular basis? How is your **health**?" Through these questions, I have reduced life's experiences

ASK
Always
Seek
Knowledge

LIFE
Love
Is
For
Everyone

FUN
Forget
Unnecessary
Nonsense

HUMOR
Help
Undo
My
Ordinary
Response

GIFT
Good
Intentions
For
Things

TALENT
To
Achieve,
Latent
Energy
Needs
Training

HEALTH
Hopefully
Everyone
Accesses
Life's
Trip
Happily

to three simple words. I call these life's expectations or the three *L-Es* of life: Levity, Legacy, and Longevity.

The legendary Curt Gowdy has been called the smooth voice of sports history. He announced Ted Williams' last at bat, which, of course, was a home run; the first Super Bowl; decades of All Star baseball games; many World Series games; and the Montreal Olympics. He also hosted *The American Sportsman*, which became one of the most popular outdoor television series of all time.

When Curt was asked how he saw himself as an announcer, he said, "I tried to pretend that I was sitting in the stands with a buddy, watching the game, poking him in the ribs when something exciting happened. I never took myself too seriously." Here's what John Wooden, the famous basketball coach from UCLA, said about him: "Curt Gowdy was just highly respected and well thought of, not just as a sportscaster, but as a person."

Curt lived to the enviable age of eighty-six. What a great example of someone who was able to fulfill his life's expectations—to enjoy life, to affect many people with his gifts and talents, and to live a long time to accomplish those things. A perfect example of how to fulfill the three *L-Es*: Levity, Legacy, and Longevity!

CAN
Character
Advances
Nobility

What would you like to change in your life so you **can** have a better chance of reaching your expectations? Let's heed the advice of Henry David Thoreau (1817–1862), an American writer who said, "Things do not change; we change."

Here we go . . .

CHAPTER 2

HONESTY

<u>H</u>elping <u>O</u>thers <u>N</u>otice <u>E</u>ach <u>S</u>ituation <u>T</u>ruthfully

While I was serving on a **team** of school district administrators, our responsibility was to deliver the services to schools to enable the staffs to meet their students' needs. We set goals, established strategies, analyzed our limitations, and proceeded in good **faith** to fulfill those **goals**.

TEAM
Tolerance
Empowers
All
Members

To accomplish those goals, we determined that what we needed most from the people we were serving was their honesty. The ultimate success of delivering a quality education to 13,000 students was based on the honesty of the staff and administrators we were working with. I discovered that maintaining healthy working **relationships** that encourage honesty is much like visiting a doctor.

FAITH
Forget
All
Insecurities;
Trust
Hope

If you are ill and go to the doctor, you will explain the details of your ailment. Your doctor will ask you a series of questions, and you will **respond** as best you can. Your doctor's questions might even lead you to **ask** other questions yourself. Your doctor will diagnose the problem and, hopefully, provide a remedy for your ailment. In this scenario, honesty will obviously be the best policy.

GOALS
Greatness
Only
Awaits
Labor—
Staaaaaart

Do you think that honesty is always the **best** policy? No, no way, reconsider, definitely not, huh-uh, are you kidding, nope, certainly not, not always, not on your life buoy! Why do I react to this question with such an emphatic no?

Honesty is the best policy, **if** you are honest with yourself in deciding what the best policy is

RELATIONSHIPS
Realizing
Every
Love,
Attaining
Truth
In
Our
Negative
Situations,
Helps
Individuals
Produce
Satisfaction

RESPOND
Respecting
Every
Statement
People
Offer
Needs
Diligence

ASK
Always
Seek
Knowledge

BEST
Beautiful
Endeavors
Seem
Terrific

regarding honesty. Let's study that statement again: Honesty is the best policy, if you are honest with yourself in deciding what the best policy is regarding honesty. Are you confused yet?

How do you define honesty? Do you define honesty as divulging all of the facts that you know? Or, do you define honesty as divulging only the facts that need to be known. Do you consider the feelings of the recipient of the facts? Do you remain within the **rules** and **laws**? Are the people judging those rules and laws being honest?

Imagine Dennis the Menace, the cartoon character, saying to his little friend Margaret as she was putting on her make up, "If that stuff is supposed to make you beautiful, it's not working!" Was Dennis being totally honest about his opinion? Sure he was. Did he consider Margaret's feelings or reactions? Duh!

When someone gives you a compliment, should you disagree with them? Think of the times that you have offered someone a compliment and the recipient did not accept it gracefully. Were they in fact calling you a liar? Let me share my lesson in learning how to accept honest compliments with **dignity**.

Those of us majoring in music at Central Washington University were required to study private lessons and to perform regularly at public recitals. Many of us loved this opportunity to display our passion for making music. During my college years, I was concentrating on singing and playing a euphonium, which is also referred to as a baritone horn.

The more technically advanced I became on my horn; the more difficult it became to **improve**.

Consequently, in an effort to continue improving, I was spending up to five hours a day attached to my instrument. I was on a rigorous personal practice schedule, in addition to performing with several different organizations. The harder I worked, the more my ego expanded and the tougher it got to accept anything except absolute perfection. Here's what Vince Lombardi, the infamous football coach of the Greenbay Packers football team, said about this calamity of working: "There is no substitute; the harder you work, the harder it is to lose."

Mr. Robert Panerio, my extremely enthusiastic, fantastic private brass teacher, and I had worked very hard perfecting a piece written by Earnest Williams entitled "The Fifth Concerto for Trumpet." It is common to play a piece on a different instrument, and I was to perform it on my baritone horn. The piece consists of three movements, or sections, and takes about thirty minutes to perform in its entirety. Not only did I have it perfected, I had it memorized!

I performed this incredibly difficult piece at a public recital on campus. During the performance, two small spots weren't absolutely perfect. At the conclusion of the piece, I bowed to the audience and retreated from the stage. I was furious with myself; absolute perfection was my goal, and it had eluded me.

My voice teacher, Mrs. Mary Elizabeth Whitner, was waiting offstage to enter and accompany one of her students in a vocal solo. As I departed the stage, she smiled and very kindly said, "Marvelous job, Bruce." I muttered something unintelligible to her and continued stomping off the stage.

The next day, Mrs. Whitner asked to meet with me. I will never forget that meeting. The Jell-O really

IF
Initiate
Fantasies

RULES
Regulating
Us
Leads
Everyone to
Success

LAW
Learn
Allowable
Ways

DIGNITY
Depicting
Integrity
Granting
Nobility
In
Thy
Years

IMPROVE
Individuals
Make
Progress
Rewarding
Our
Valiant
Efforts

RUDE
Really
Useless
Defensive
Endeavors

RIGHT
Respecting
Individuals
Grants
Honor
Today

EGOTIST
Everybody
Gags
On
The
Individual's
Selfish
Traits

ACTIONS
Allowing
Change
Towards
Improvement
Offers
Needed
Success

SMILE
Sure
Makes
It
Lots
Easier

hit the fan. She explained to me, in no uncertain terms, that she had been absolutely honest with me in offering a compliment the previous evening at the recital. She very emphatically pointed out that she was thrilled with my performance and that she expected an apology from me because of the **rude** manner in which I reacted to her compliment. Her tirade continued for nearly an hour. She was **right**.

In striving for perfection to fulfill the goal of bolstering my ego, I had neglected to fully appreciate my own accomplishments and the importance of the relationships with my mentors. Had my ego gotten in the way of my honest appraisal of my accomplishments? Had my ego gotten in the way of my relationship with Mrs. Whitner? Do you think that I had reacted like an **egotist**? Mrs. Whitner, I would like to thank you again for your honest appraisal of my inappropriate **actions**.

Is it possible to disagree with someone sharing an honest compliment without hurting that person's feelings? Many years ago our youngest son, Dave, and I were shopping in a local store. His long curly locks were in desperate need of their first trim. A very kind sales associate approached us with a loving **smile** and delivered a compliment that was truly the definition of a "double whammy."

She said, "Oh, such a cute baby. How old is your granddaughter?" I immediately remembered my tongue lashing from Mrs. Whitner about receiving honest compliments. I replied, "Thank you for your **kind** words; the baby is six months old."

Think of all of the other things I could have said to her. What would the point have been to say something that would have embarrassed her? Was my response honest? Did I need to prove my honesty by providing more information regarding the baby in that statement? No!

While I was in college, a Northwest solo contest was held at the Festival of Roses in Portland, Oregon. University musicians from several states competed at the event. The winner of the solo contest was to receive a substantial cash prize plus the honor of performing for thousands of people at a Festival of Roses event. The music faculty at Central Washington University encouraged me to represent their institution at the contest. It was a tremendous opportunity to receive recognition for my years of hard work. At that point, I had totally perfected the magnificent thirty-minute piece I mentioned earlier, and I was ready to win the contest.

My performance at the event was absolutely flawless. The audience erupted in an earth-shattering ovation; everyone knew the euphonium player from Central Washington University was going to collect all the accolades. After listening to the rest of the competitors, we were convinced that if the judges were honest, I would definitely be selected as the **winner**.

The winner was announced. It was an instrumentalist from a different university. Nobody could believe it, especially me. I was so emotionally distraught that I immediately left the performance area without my horn.

Did I make an honest assessment of my performance? Did I listen to the other competitors' performances? Was the audience expecting me to be selected? Was the person selected as the winner a private lesson student of the adjudicator? Did I

KIND
Keep
It
Nice
Dear

WINNER
We
Interrupt
Negativism
Now
Everyone
Reaches
Success

have a reason to be upset? The answer to all these questions is yes.

Was the contest organized in an honest manner? You decide!

Did the judge make an honest selection? You decide!

Did I return to retrieve my instrument? After a U-turn.

Recently, Bill Gates of Microsoft helped me continue on my road to recovery by saying to his employees: "Life isn't fair; get over it." Does Mr. Gates's statement indicate that people are dishonest and, sometimes, to preserve our mental stability, we need to learn to let go of our **egos**? Yes!

Dr. Wayne Hertz, the choir director and music department chairman at Central Washington University, once said; "Anybody can **complain**, but it takes someone with an **idea** for improvement to make a difference." With the memories of that painful solo contest experience forever emblazoned on my mind, I set out on a mission to improve the fairness of future music contests.

When I became an administrator, I accepted an invitation to produce a booklet describing the steps for organizing and facilitating music contests. After the booklet was published, I was asked to invent a method of adjudicating choirs, which I did. I have been told that both these publications have been distributed far and wide to help thousands and thousands of people in helping keep honesty in the forefront of judging music contests.

Do you think Mr. Gates and Dr. Hertz would approve of my efforts to help participants of music contests be treated fairly? Are there things in your

EGOS
Everybody
Greedily
Owns
Some

COMPLAIN
Carefully
Object—
Making
People
Listen
Aggravates
Individuals
Needlessly

IDEA
Inspiration
Deserves
Everyone's
Attention

world that you could help change to assist others in ensuring honesty?

How many times do we say things to people in total honesty that get us into trouble? Lots and lots and lots of times and lots of trouble. Total honesty easily leads to insults and confrontations. A friend of mine recently commented on my hair. He said, "Before you go on that television show you certainly should get an extreme makeover on your hair." Was he being honest? Did he hurt my feelings? Kinda. My reaction was simple: "I know."

I could have said lots of things. I could have been very honest and said that my regular hair cutter was on vacation when I got my hair cut a month ago. I could have countered that my friend probably wished that he had a TV show to worry about. I could have been really cruel and said, "At least I have hair to **worry** about."

Was I honest about not divulging all of the facts? Yes, I was honest with myself because I view our friendship as much more important then the facts surrounding the last time I was butchered in the barber chair. Did he know the facts? No! Did he need to know the facts? No! Does my ego need to be fulfilled by the hair follicle police force? No!

How many times do we attempt to "be honest" with someone when our only intention is to be noticed? When we are honest can we open ourselves up to unfair criticism?

Several years ago on a dark, rainy night, I was driving on a very busy street near our home. I noticed a small white dog standing by another dog lying on the side the road. I stopped to investigate. Sadly, it was apparent that the dog lying on the

WORRY
Wickedness
Only
Result'n
Resentment
Y'know

pavement had just been hit by a car and had expired. As I was investigating, the other little dog raced off to a nearby house. I picked up the fatally injured dog and carried him to the house, where his canine companion was scratching on the door.

I sorrowfully informed the people who came to the door that I had found their pet alongside the road, and he had apparently been struck by a car. The people thanked me for bringing their deceased dog to their house. As I drove away, I knew the people did not believe that I had simply found the dead dog. I knew they believed I had run over their dog, which I did not do. I was honest with myself; that's what counted.

It turned out that our two boys told the story to their friends the next day at their daycare center. When I picked them up that afternoon, they told me that the dog I had found alongside the road the previous night belonged to one of the children at their daycare. The little boy at the day care told my sons, Jeff and Dave, "The dog your dad ran over and killed last night was mine." My sons and I had a long talk about being honest whether others believe us or not.

Had I been honest with the owners of the dog? Yes. Did they **believe** me? No. Had they shared their honest feelings with their little boy? Yes. Did they need to share their honest feelings with their small child? No. Did I **feel** horrible? Yes! Would I react exactly the same way in the future to prove my honesty to myself? Yes!

Years ago, I called my father to wish him happy holidays. My wife and I were with our sons celebrating the holidays at her parents' home 300 miles

BELIEVE
Bountiful
Experiences
Loved
If
Everyone
Visualizes
Eventualities

FEEL
Faith
Eventually
Elevates
Love

from my father's house. He was having trouble speaking because of a tremendous amount of pain he was experiencing in his abdomen. I called my brother and sisters and informed them of his plight and pleaded with them to encourage him to rush to an emergency room.

We left as soon as possible to be at my father's side. He had been diagnosed with a perforated ulcer in his intestines. The excruciating pain he was experiencing was the result of several quarts of acidic fluid leaking from his digestive tract into his abdomen.

As the days passed, Dad's condition continued to deteriorate. It was apparent that, because of other system failures, his perforated ulcer was not going to heal. His doctors sadly informed us that his condition was terminal.

Dad was attached to a ventilator, and while his life was slipping away, our family pondered a very difficult decision. Should we be totally honest with him and explain that he was not going to recover from his perforated ulcer? Or should we give him the impression that there was **hope** for his recovery?

We decided to be honest with ourselves regarding Dad's impending death but not to inform him that he was about to die. Because of the tubes in his body, it was impossible for him to converse. We decided that due to his intense suffering, the realization of his impending death would have only added to his suffering. To this day, I feel that, in his case, our family made the **right** decision.

Reaching the end of life's journey in every situation is unique; Mom's last few days were totally different from Dad's. Because of her afflictions due

HOPE
Harnessing
Optimism
Produces
Empowerment

RIGHT
Respecting
Individuals
Grants
Honor
Today

PEACE
Practicing
Effective
Attitudes
Calms
Everyone

RULES
Regulating
Us
Leads
Everyone to
Success

LAW
Learn
Allowable
Ways

HELP
Hurry
Everyone
Loves
Progress

FREEDOM
Forget
Restrictions
Enjoy
Every
Days's
Opportunistic
Moments

to smoking, she knew that her breathing was going to soon be over. She resigned herself to accepting her final moments on this earth. I have very fond memories of our last hours together. The opportunity for the honest assessment of her health was a very loving conversation that I'll remember forever. She had decided that she was tired of battling to stay alive and that it was time for her to seek **peace** with her maker.

Can we apply these same characteristics of honesty in our everyday lives? Can we apply them throughout our society and in our business endeavors?

Our societies have established **rules** and **laws** in an attempt to **help** us practice honesty with others. Nearly everything that we do is restricted so our **freedom** will not infringe upon the rights of others. In **reality**, our level of honesty is measured in everything we do.

There are legal consequences if we lie, cheat, steal, avoid taxes, drive too fast, slander someone, compete unfairly, display hate, display disrespect, make threats, hit someone, hurt someone, etc., etc., etc. When you analyze this list, do you realize that almost everything that we consider bad is simply not being realistic in fulfilling our definition of honesty?

Years ago, while I was chaperoning a high school dance, I asked the police officer on duty a very simple question, "What has been the most memorable situation you have dealt with during your career?" He immediately broke into uncontrollable laughter.

When the officer began to recover from his emotional overload, he related a story of an incident that occurred before the general public had access to emergency scanning devices. While he was stopped behind a car at a traffic light, he heard a report of a robbery over his police radio. The dispatcher alerted him that a 7-Eleven store in his precinct had just been robbed by four men who had escaped in a four-door sedan. He happened to notice that the car in front of him was a sedan containing four men.

The traffic light turned green, and the four-door sedan failed to proceed through the intersection. When the traffic light switched back to red, the officer activated his emergency lights and began walking towards the sedan to ask the driver if he was having a mechanical problem.

As he approached the car, a fellow in the back seat hurriedly rolled down his window, stuck his head out, and started yelling, "We didn't rob that 7-Eleven Store; we didn't rob that 7-Eleven Store!" The four people were promptly arrested, and the robbery was solved just minutes after it occurred— long before it was ever reported in the newspaper, on television, or on the radio.

Do you think this escapade taught those four individuals several lessons? Were the robbers reminded in a big hurry that stealing is against the law? Were they reminded that being **arrested** and carted off to jail can be a serious consequence of breaking the law? Did the fellow in the back seat develop a new opinion regarding the old adage that states, "Honesty is always the best policy?"

If someone is dishonest, we define that as telling a **lie**. That lie will probably fall into one of two categories. It will be "a little white lie," commonly called a **fib**, which usually doesn't hurt any-

REALITY
Recognizing
Eventualities,
Accepting
Life's
Inequities
Teaches
You

ARREST
A
Required
Reservation
Employing
Selfdiscipline
Training

LIE
Losers
Intentionally
Exaggerate

FIB
Facts
Intentionally
Bent

LUCK
Languishing
Using
Current
Knowledge

FUN
Forget
Unnecessary
Nonsense

BLUFF
Believable
Lies
Undermine
Faith
Forever

one. Or it will be a serious lie, which is often pre-meditated and can maliciously end a career, a relationship, a marriage, or a life.

When I was about twenty-five years old, I was fishing for steelhead trout in a small stream near my home. Early one morning, **luck** shined down and a beautiful chrome-bright fish, about ten pounds, grabbed my lure. Playing this huge sea-going rainbow trout was so much **fun**! Throughout the battle, my mouth was watering, imagining biting into an alder-fire-cooked filet of fresh trout. I wrestled her to the beach and ran her up to my car and quickly hid my treasure in the trunk.

It was legal to catch fish from that small stream; however, I didn't want any other fisherman to witness my success. The limit was two fish per day. Many times, steelhead travel in matched pairs, so my heart was pounding in anticipation of connecting with her traveling companion.

Just after I closed the trunk, a fellow I didn't know very well named Jerry drove up, got out of his car and said, "Top o' the mornin' ta ya Bruce; have any luck?" As you might expect, I became all tongue tied and tried to **bluff** him by launching into a little white lie. I sheepishly said, "Nope, I guess the fish just haven't started to migrate up here yet. Sure is a nice day, but I haven't had any action in this stream for a long, long time."

Did I want Jerry to know that I had a fish in the trunk? Of course not! I was afraid that if he knew about the fish in my trunk he would go down to the stream and catch the other one. After he finally drove away, I scurried back down to the same spot and hooked another beautiful fish. That one did not end up in my trunk . . . he got away.

Years later, after I became good friends with Jerry, we discussed the meeting we had at that small stream. We became consumed with raucous laughter. Jerry explained that he knew the fish was in my trunk . . . he could hear it flopping!

Did I lie? Sure. Did Jerry understand why I lied? Sure. Would I do the same thing if I were to be in the same situation again? Probably! Now those times are just pleasant memories. The stream is no longer open for fishing at that time of the year; I got married and sold that beautiful car. Don't worry, you'll be able to tell which green Pontiac GTO was parked near that stream; I'm sure it still smells like fish!

A couple of years ago I had a set of new heavy-duty tires installed on my three-quarter-ton pickup truck that carries a camper. Then I proceeded to an express lube station to have my aging truck serviced. As I was killing time in the waiting room, I struck up a conversation with a very pleasant young lady. During our conversation, she explained how she was having a tough financial struggle because she was working to support herself while she was attending classes at a nearby college. We discussed her goals, and I complimented her on her aspirations to graduate from college and become a schoolteacher.

She explained that she was very concerned that one of the tires on her car was low on air. However, she read on the list of services hanging on the wall that checking the tire pressure was part of the service package she had agreed to pay for. I said, "If you were my daughter, I'd encourage you to go to the tire store where I just purchased my new tires. They will check your low tire and fix it for free. Driving on the freeway with a bad tire can be

TRUST
Thoroughly
Relying
Upon
Someone's
Tenacity

MAD
Meanness
Always
Destroys

FACT
Finding
Actual
Circumstances
True

ANGER
Acclaiming
Negative
Garbage
Eradicates
Relationships

a life-threatening experience." She pointed out that she had a lot of **trust** in the technicians who were servicing her car to check the air pressure.

A technician invited her to the counter and summarized the service that had supposedly been completed on her car. He assured her that the tire pressure checked out at thirty-five pounds per tire, the manufacturer's recommended pressure. The young lady paid the bill, retrieved her keys, thanked him, and headed for the freeway.

The time arrived for me to pay. The technician summarized the service my pickup received and mentioned that my tire pressure, just like the lady's, was fine. He said the pressure checked out to be thirty-five pounds per tire. Does that seem strange to you? It did to me.

I kept telling myself, "don't get **mad**; just get the **facts**. My message to them will not be nearly as effective if my **anger** overshadows the lesson they are about to receive." I asked, "Are you sure that my tire pressure and that young lady's tire pressure both check out to be the same?" He assured me that every detail of their company's policy was followed during the service on both vehicles.

I said, "You know that I'm planning on paying my bill . . . just after all four of you who are working here bring an air pressure gauge and check the air in my tires. I would like you to prove that I have thirty-five pounds of air in each tire." The entire crew and I checked the truck's air pressure. Each tire contained seventy pounds of air pressure.

Those four technicians were the recipients of a very intense lesson from a very angry former customer. I pointed out to them that the lady who just left was headed for a long trip on the freeway, and they had lied to her about the safety of the tires her life depended on.

Did the technicians intentionally omit some steps in the service to minimize the time they spent on each vehicle so the company could make more money? Was the lady in danger because of their dishonest maintenance?

This is just a small example of how lies and deception to reap financial gain can harm a company's reputation. If the company's reputation is harmed, can its **profits** eventually suffer?

Was I a part of the lie? Yes, I was part of their lie because I failed to report their deceptive business practices to an independent organization or to an official of their franchised business. So in essence, by not reporting their omission of checking the air pressure, I condoned it.

Robert Lewis Stevenson, British essayist, novelist and poet, said, "The cruelest lies are often told in silence." If we know someone is lying in a situation that has the potential of hurting someone emotionally or physically, is it our ethical responsibility to intercede? Should we shine the light of truth to enable the situation to be rectified? Is the primary person we need to be honest with currently wearing our clothing?

Were the car technicians, in essence, robbing from the poor and giving to the rich? Could this be called the opposite of the Robin Hood principle? Do you remember that Robin Hood stole from the rich and gave to the poor? So, what if we call the car technicians' actions the "Hobin Rood" principle? They were stealing from the poor and giving to the

PROFITS
Providing
Revenue
Opportunities
Fulfills
Individual
Tasks
Successfully

rich. Do many individuals and organizations conduct business this way? Simply study news reports and analyze why people are incarcerated, and you will understand the answer to that question.

How should we react if someone labels us as dishonest by calling us a liar? Is staying away from water the safest way to avoid drowning? Is being aware of the limit and not breaking it the best way to avoid a ticket from a fisheries officer for catching too many fish? Is staying within the speed limit the best way to avoid a speeding ticket? Are you starting to get the picture?

During my second year of teaching, I was the band director at Peninsula High School in Gig Harbor, Washington. A fellow teacher stopped me in the hall one day and said, "Bruce, you aren't supposed to smoke cigarettes on school grounds; you know that's against school district rules, and you could be fired." I gulped and asked, "Why do you need to tell me that?" He said, "I saw you step out of your new green Pontiac GTO yesterday, wearing your beige overcoat and you walked towards the building while you were smoking a cigarette."

I had a simple response. "That could not have been me; I was not smoking on campus yesterday. For openers, I have never taken a puff from a cigarette in my entire life!" He violently disagreed and elaborated that he was absolutely sure that was me and if he saw me smoking on campus again he would report me to the principal. Because it was very apparent he had his mind made up, I was dumbfounded. The only response I could muster was something like "I'm **sorry** you have that impression."

SORRY
Success
Often
Requires
Rescinding
Yourself

Was there any need to argue? Certainly not, it would have been a waste of my breath and his time.

The fingers on one of my hands provide more digits than I need to count the times in my life when I have been at a loss for words. But, I started counting just after that discussion. He was absolutely certain that he had witnessed me smoking on campus. I have never smoked a cigarette in my life, and I don't have a twin or a clone.

Was I being honest? Absolutely.

Was he calling me a liar? Absolutely.

Was I the person who knew the truth? Absolutely.

Was it worth my emotional energy to report him to the principal? Absolutely not.

Was it worth my emotional energy to argue with him? Absolutely not.

Did I ask him if the GTO smelled like fish? I should have!

The major reason to avoid lying, cheating, stealing, breaking rules and laws is those actions' boomerang affect. The knowledge of having broken the trust of others is a huge burden to bear. Feelings of shame and guilt can damage a person's feelings of self-worth beyond repair. This can lead to a lifetime of anguish, anxiety, and uncertainty because of the loss of the most precious gift we can possess . . . self-respect!

Robert Lewis Stevenson sums up the need for honesty very succinctly:

> "What hangs people most . . . is the unfortunate circumstance of guilt."

CHAPTER 3

ATTITUDE

All Terrific Thoughts Incorporate Terrific Unrelenting Dedication to Excellence

Your attitude,
Not your aptitude
Will develop your altitude
And your attitude of gratitude
Will affect your latitude—helping avoid ineptitude.

Would you like to list the people that you really enjoy being around because you like their attitude? Are you saying that you enjoy being in their presence because they are almost always positive and associating with them just makes you feel good?

Does this prove how important it is to remain positive in our communications with others? Isn't that simple?

The majority of the earth's surface is covered with water; that's a good thing. Water is the foundation for the protoplasm in all living things. The food we grow needs it; we wash our bodies and clothing in it; we drink it, put it in our food, and use it to fight fires. We swim in it, fish in it, and go water skiing, jet skiing, and wake boarding in it. We also race boats in it, go kayaking, sailing, and cruising in it. The majority of the world's commerce uses water as a highway for the distribution of goods. Water is great stuff . . . if our heads are above the surface!

Can we view our attitudes much like we view water? We use water in a plethora of positive ways for our mere existence as human beings. However, water can also have a devastating negative effect on us. Thousands of humans drown each year due to swimming accidents, boating accidents, floods, tsunamis, and other disasters. Water also carries deadly diseases that kill thousands of people and animals annually. Water has positive and negative effects—just like our attitudes.

Do you wish to spend your lifetime freely enjoying the positive benefits of the surface of the water, or do you want to spend your time fighting for air because you are sinking with a negative attitude? Let's take a look at how our lives are influenced by our attitudes.

Do you think that most of our thoughts are positive or negative? People who study thought processes have discovered that our subconscious minds produce about seventy-five percent negative thoughts. I know, you're probably thinking, "I know some so and so's who certainly let their subconscious do most of the talking for them."

How do we avoid falling into the trap of being one of those "so and so's?" You know the type of person I'm talking about, someone who is so negative that nobody wants to be around them. Maybe a much better question might be: How do we get out of the trap of thinking and talking from a negative perspective? All of us fight this battle at different levels as we swim through life, just as we try to keep our head above the surface of the water when we wear our swimming suits.

Let's create a simple exercise to help us visualize the use of positive and negative responses in our speech processes. What if we spell from the top down a word that has to do with the concept of paying attention to our speech patterns? For this simple exercise we will use the word **focus**. And what if we use this word as an acronym to help us develop **positive** thought patterns and avoid **negative** patterns of **response**?

Faith	F	Fear
Opportunity	O	Obligation
Care	C	Confrontation
Understanding	U	Useless
Success	S	Screaming

Would you like the *F* in focus to stand for **faith** in ourselves and one another to meet the challenges set out before us? Or would you rather live under the cloud of **fear** and be forced to react? In other words, would you rather be trusted and valued or belittled and unduly criticized?

I was once a member of a choir that had a visiting director who was totally negative. As soon as he stepped in front of the choir, we sounded horrible and we sang terribly out of tune. I'll never forget the day he **yelled** at us that he knew we were going to sing out of tune even before we began singing! Think of the people you know who inhibit your productivity in this same manner. Is this because of their lack of faith in themselves and in you, displayed by their negative attitude? Do you have an allergic reaction to negativism? I certainly do!

Volumes and volumes have been written on the topic of faith, and the best-selling book of all time is about faith. Our perceptions of spiritualism at the mention of the word *faith* are as varied as the number of people on this planet. For our purposes, let's

FOCUS
Faith,
Opportunity,
Care,
Unconditional
Understanding,
Success

Fear,
Obligation,
Confrontation,
Useless,
Screaming

POSITIVE
Please
Offer
Sincere
Insights
To
Instill
Values
Effectively

NEGATIVE
Never
Enjoy
Goodness
Always
Treat
Individuals
Very
Egotistically

RESPONSE
Respect
Every
Statement
People
Offer
Never
Seem
Egotistical

FAITH
Forget
All
Insecurities;
Trust
Hope

FEAR
Freezes
Every
Action....
Reconsider

YELL
You
Eventually
Lose
Love

CANDO
Courage
Always
Necessitates
Developing
Opportunities

analyze the **can do** aspect of the word. Webster defines faith as "allegiance to duty or a person: **Loyalty** . . . complete confidence."

How about the *O* in the word **focus**? Do you have to be where you are today? Do you have to be doing all the things in your life that you don't enjoy doing? Carl A., Carl B., Joey H., Karen S., Rick M., Cathy S., Paul M., Dana M., Freddie M., and Mike M. would love to trade places with you. Would they view your daily responsibilities as obligations?

"Who are these people you listed?" you ask. If you wanted to trade places, I could guarantee they would view their new responsibilities as magnificent opportunities. You see, they are all former students of mine who have passed away, some while attending high school. Should we view our lives and our pursuits as obligations or opportunities?

What if the *C* in **focus** stands for displaying how much we care about ourselves and others? For your benefit, please say the first two syllables of the word *character* out loud. Will this help you remember that character simply means, "Do you **care** how you **act**?"

What happens to our lives if the *C* stands for confrontation? Do you spend your time arguing and fighting with others in an attempt to prove your superiority? Does your envy towards others surface via your judgmental assessments? Does your jealousy evolve into unfairly criticizing and tearing others down to build up your own ego? Do you employ these forms of negativism to try to prove that you are better than others because you are an **egotist**? Can you think of people who **tease** and **bully** others so they can feed their own egos? Can this drama of an ego feeding frenzy very easily lead to emotional and physical harm?

While I was a very small seventh grader, a very unpleasant incident occurred on an afternoon bus ride home from school. An extremely large ninth grader named Alton decided he was going to show his friends how he could tease and bully me. We were seated in the back of the bus as he began displaying his superiority to bolster his ego. He began teasing and bullying me while punching me in the face. Alton made it very clear that if I cried for help he would continue wailing on me after I got off the bus. I was terrified. I sat there and took it! I will never forget our bus driver Mr. Pickering's look of shock and horror when he saw the blood gushing from my face as I walked past him to exit the bus. Even though my nose really hurt, I felt more pain for our beloved bus driver than for myself.

Mr. Pickering asked me what had just happened; I reluctantly recounted the events of the incident. He then launched into a very intense discussion with Alton and later reported him to Mr. Hinderlie, our junior high school principal.

Do you think Alton would have beaten me up if we were the only students on the bus? Of course not; he was only showing off for his friends. You would probably agree that the best way to break up a fight is to leave the combatants alone so they have no one to entertain. Why didn't I alert the bus driver during the punch out? I was embarrassed that I couldn't protect myself, and I was also extremely intimidated by Alton's threats. Did I strike back? Of course not, I knew that fighting was breaking the rules.

LOYALTY
Life
Offers
You
All
Levels,
Trust
Yours

CARE
Courage
Always
Resonates
Endearingly

ACT
Always
Carefully
Tread

EGOTIST
Everybody
Gags
On
The
Individual's
Selfish
Traits

TEASE
To
Enjoy
Abuse
Signifies
Evil

BULLY
Brashness
Ultimately
Lessens
Loving
You

HONESTY
Helping
Others
Notice
Every
Situation
Truthfully

SMILE
Sure
Makes
It
Lots
Easier

THANKS
To
Honestly
Acknowledge
Noble
Kindness
Shown

How many situations have you experienced that have involved teasing, bullying, embarrassment, intimidation, and harassment? Too many? Should you have sought help? Certainly! Should I have informed Mr. Pickering? Did he feel horrible that he wasn't aware of my predicament? Did I feel horrible that I hadn't informed my friend, Mr. Pickering?

One of the simplest ways to start a confrontation is simply to ask a question to which the response might be less than **honest**. Years ago when I was a very young teacher, a student was sitting in the back of a class with a freshly peeled orange in her hand. A pile of orange peels was under her chair. So, with eighty high school students as witnesses, I posed an innocent question from the front of the room. I asked, "Are those your orange peels under your chair?"

She unequivocally said, "No."

You would not believe how that simple question started a confrontation that escalated beyond your wildest imagination . . . all the way to the principal's office. I had asked a straightforward question in front of eighty people assuming that the obvious answer would result . . . wrong!

It would have been so simple to have just walked up to her with a **smile** on my face and whispered, "That orange looks absolutely delicious. But please save it for later, and make sure you deposit those peels in the trash when class is over. You're wonderful. **Thanks**!"

Is it the goals that we attempt to achieve or the attitudes of others we are forced to endure that help us decide which involvements we elect to pursue in the future? One more time... Is it the goals that we attempt to achieve or the attitudes of others we are forced to endure that help us decide which involvements we elect to pursue in the future?

Here's a less serious example of how questioning works. When I'm about to hop into the shower, I ask my wife, Mary Ann, this simple question, and she always responds with the same answer, "Well do you think I'll make myself beautiful by taking a shower?" She retorts, "I'm not sure we have that much water."

What if the *U* in the word *focus* stands for useless? How do we respond when someone calls us useless? While I was in high school, my grades plummeted from being on the honor roll to struggling to pass my classes. My parents were in the middle of a horrendous battle that culminated in a divorce when I was sixteen years old. It was understandably very difficult to concentrate on schoolwork when my mind was consumed with the **worries** regarding my family's future and my personal security.

One day, a teacher was passing back quizzes to students in the class. My test arrived on my desk with a big red *F*, indicating failure, emblazoned across the top of the page. As you might imagine, I was devastated. But I was ready to **try** to do better; I was eager to hear the teacher review the test, so I could prepare for the next **test**.

This young teacher decided to use me as an example to the rest of the class. As I was very proudly sitting there in the new clothes I had purchased with money I had earned, he launched into a personal attack. He started carrying on about how so many students had flunked the test because they

WORRIES
Wickedness
Only
Results'n
Resentment
In
Every
Situation

TRY
To
Respect
Yourself

TEST
To
Evaluate
Student's
Teacher

apparently didn't care about the importance of his class in their lives. Blah, blah, blah, blah, blah, blah, blah. Then he said, "And Bruce back there thinks that the world owes him a living." I immediately went brain dead. Fortunately, I wasn't thrown out of school because of my emotional response to his cruel, unnecessary, and very unprofessional comments.

That teacher had just shared his opinion with thirty of my closest friends that I was absolutely useless.Can you imagine how my attitude toward him and that subject evolved during that class? Could he have simply walked to my desk and asked, "Bruce, your mind seems to be in lots of other places during class; would you like to stop by my classroom after school and fill me in on what seems to be bothering you?" In later years, I have asked hundreds of students questions just like the one he should have asked me. If he had asked what was bothering my concentration, he would have proven his desire for unconditional understanding, the *U* in *focus*.

Would you like the *S* in the word *focus* to stand for someone screaming at you, hoping to receive their desired response? My screaming at students began to subside when I learned what to tell them to help them improve. I'll state that again: My screaming at students began to subside when I learned what to tell them to help them improve. I no longer blatantly blamed them for doing things wrong; I simply learned how to explain doing things right. John Wooden, the legendary UCLA basketball coach, says, "A person may make mistakes, but he isn't a failure until he starts blaming someone else."

We all respect leaders who possess the knowledge and the wisdom to impart their knowledge to others. Empowerment is the key to leading others to **success**, which is the *S* in the word *focus*. Now, take the time to list other words, beginning with the letters of the word *focus*, which are commonly employed in the preceding context.

It is easy to have a winning attitude if everything is going as planned, and success is a result of dedication and hard work. How do we deal with a situation where a poisonous attitude attempts to destroy our route to success?

One day as I was on my way from the parking lot at Clover Park High School to enter the door near the choir room, I noticed a ballpoint pen lying in the mud. I stooped down to pick it up but decided to leave it there; the pen was just too muddy to bother with.

Nearly every morning before school, I stood outside the music room door and greeted the students as they passed by in the hallway. I loved that part of the day, greeting hundreds of students carrying their possessions to their first class and being around the bountiful enthusiasm of youth was so much **fun**. This particular day, I said hi to Bubba as he was walking down the hallway towards the locker room carrying his gym bag.

Since my preparation period was about to start, I walked out of that building to Mr. Thomas's room in the adjoining wing of the school. Within moments of my arrival in my fishing buddy's classroom, Matt looked out the window and exclaimed, "Look! The school is on fire!"

We could see a small ribbon of smoke emitting from the vent in the laundry room near the gym. Students began running out of that part of the building. I raced across the passageway to investigate. I

SUCCESS
Seek
Understanding
Carefully
Character
Eventually
Sows
Satisfaction

FUN
Forget
Unnecessary
Nonsense

REALITIES
Recognizing
Eventualities,
Accepting
Life's
Inequities
Teaches
You

ACCEPT
All
Circumstances
Can
Eventually
Produce
Truth

HEROES
Help
Everyone
Regardless
Of
Encountering
Stress

ran into the hallway near the choir room, yelled into the black curtain of smoke to see if anyone was still in the building, and then escaped back outside.

The fire alarms were sounding, and everyone was screaming as the students and staff ran for safety. A heart-wrenching question spread quickly through the assembled crowd: Where's Lola? We could not locate her. We were horrified. Lola was blind. After what seemed an eternity, magnificent news traveled throughout the crowd of displaced people—Lola had been located!

Hundreds of students were standing outside watching a third of the building, including the choir room, being consumed by a ravenous blaze. We were shocked by the ferocious fiery onslaught on our beloved school. Everything happened so fast. About five minutes after we noticed the first wisp of smoke, a bone-chilling crash signaled the collapse of the gym roof.

A very dedicated choir student named Dan looked at me in shock and through his tears said "Mr. B., you aren't crying." I calmly said, "Dan there are some **realities** in life that you just have to **accept**."

The Lakewood firefighters did a tremendous job of extinguishing the blaze and saving two-thirds of the school building. They were truly our **heroes**. The students were bused back home without their belongings, and we began searching for emergency spaces to house our displaced classes.

The community immediately offered us assistance. The choirs adopted a nearby church social hall for our rehearsal space. We loved it. The room had great acoustics, a beautiful setting, and was devoid of the distractions of the main school campus. In the two weeks immediately following the fire, we competed in a league solo contest, staged an all-school variety show, and performed at a statewide choral contest. How did we do? **Great**!

An investigation uncovered the fact that Bubba, the student I had greeted the morning of the fire, had been upset because of a conflict he was experiencing at school. He elected to display his negative attitude in a horrific manner. His gym bag contained a can of gasoline that he had ignited on the stage of the gym just as the bell was sounding to start classes for the day. Fortunately, no one was injured or killed in the incident, or Bubba would have spent even more time incarcerated for the manner in which he had elected to display his **hate**.

Several days after the disaster, the school staff was allowed to enter the hulk of the burned-out building. As I approached the door, my eyes surveyed the ground in front of the steps; the now trodden, muddy ballpoint pen was still there—reminding me once again that the more things change, the more they can remain the same; it just depends on our attitude.

GREAT
Golden
Rule
Elevates
All
Teams

HATE
Hurtful
Attitudes
Test
Everyone

CHAPTER 4

RESPECT

Recognizing Everyone's Strengths
Produces Exceptional Caring Teams

Beginning in a new school, a new living arrangement, a new job, or a new group of any kind is understandably very stressful. Some good advice to heed regarding starting anew is to keep one priority at the top of your list: Just hang on. Avoid trying to immediately change everything and everybody; just hang on. It takes time to learn the strengths of your team members and for you to earn credibility with them; just hang on. A monumental discovery that I made during my first year of teaching was realizing how much perseverance I needed to exhibit before my new students displayed respect to me.

My fellow students and I spent thousands of hours in college learning and practicing aspects of becoming outstanding music educators. We studied musical theories, educational philosophies, educational practices, human psychology, science, English, literature, math, and other subjects in addition to practicing and performing music. We did all this in a valiant effort to develop techniques for imparting our vast musical knowledge to our future students. Following this intense study and armed with my innate musical abilities, I began the journey to make my mark in the world of music education.

When I started teaching, I fell into the syndrome of blaming the students in every imaginable way for their lack of musical prowess. As a young **egotist**, it was certainly much easier for me to fix blame rather than fix the situations. My insecurities

EGOTIST
Everybody
Gags
On
The
Individual's
Selfish
Traits

REALITY
Recognizing
Eventualities,
Accepting
Life's
Inequities
Teaches
You

poured forth with insults and negativism nearly every time my lips moved.

Within my first four months of teaching, I was totally frazzled from struggling with students, parents, and coworkers. I decided to apply for a factory job to build airplanes at Boeing in Seattle. While I was standing in line to procure an application, I was struck by a severe jolt of **reality**. I thought, "It would be great to work in the human resources office here; that way I could work with people. That's what I really want to do!" I immediately departed the line without picking up an application, and I returned home to ponder my struggles in becoming a successful teacher.

After much deep thought, I finally concluded that our professors had neglected to educate us on the most important aspect of human interaction—respect. I assumed the students would respect me because I was an exceptional euphonium player; a marvelous vocalist; a flamboyant conductor; and a dashing, well-dressed, handsome dude with a hot new car—a legend in the making . . . at least in my mind! Wrong!

The students didn't give a rip about me. The one person they cared about, much to my egotistical chagrin, was themselves. How dare those selfish, impudent people not place me on a pedestal and put me first?

I finally realized that my challenge was to help students become successful from their perspective. I discovered that serving others is the only way of gaining respect in their eyes and, consequently nourishing, our self-respect.

We get what we give,
We reap what we sow,
We are the person in the mirror.

Why didn't my professors explain that to me? A much more appropriate question might be, "Was I listening when they explained it? Or was it all about me?" Sound familiar? A lump of coal placed under immense pressure for thousands of years can develop into a diamond. While under pressure, some people change into gems that sparkle like diamonds; other people simply accept acting like lumps of coal and crumble.

The length of time spent in the journey from becoming merely a lump to being a diamond in the rough and finally a gem of a person is up to each of us. The level of respect for yours truly took an abrupt about-face when I changed my concepts regarding the relationship with my students from "Me to We."

"Me!"
"I want."
"You are wrong!"
"Ha, ha, see, I told you so!"
"Why, oh why, do you even try?"
"Can't you ever do anything right?"
"I am really sorry, I was wrong."
"Can we start all over again?"
"I sure appreciate you!"
"What do you think?"
"Thank you!"
"We!"

Let's take a look at how the concept of "We" fits into relationships. The two most memorable events in most of our lives are probably being with loved ones when they enter and when they leave this world. I was fortunate to have been holding my father, Wayne's, hand when he took his final breath. It was an experience of beauty beyond belief. A peace and serenity came over him as I envisioned the bells tolling from on high. During this profound moment, I thought over and over again of what he had told me a few days earlier: "Death is the one price that we have to pay for living." Our relationship here on earth had traveled in a full circle. As I was ushering him to rest, I felt that he and I had unequivocally succeeded in life's journey to comprehend the true meaning of the word *we*.

On the opposite end of the spectrum, my wife, Mary Ann, and I were holding hands when both of our boys were born. I regret to report that this was not the beautiful, joyous experience that we were eagerly anticipating, especially for a mother screaming her lungs out as she was being racked with excruciating pain!

During both births, the babies reacted to their new world in exactly the same fashion. They immediately let everyone within earshot know that they were very unhappy about many things in their new world. They insisted on being the absolute center of their universe, and nobody else mattered—probably just like every other baby who has been born on this earth.

Do you realize that we spend the rest of our lives trying to recover from that first impression that the entire universe should revolve around us?

Most people recover; however, many of us never get over that selfish shock of leaving the comfort of the womb. Do the terms *self-centered, self-absorbed, selfish, self-interested, self-indulged, self-seeking, materialistic, my, mine, me, myself,* and *I* come to mind?

Our true self-respect is the exact reflection of the respect that we display toward others. Let's look at that concept again; the first and most important step in receiving respect is to display respect toward others. That is only possible if we can mature beyond our first impression of the world when we conclude at birth that we are the center of the universe. What can we do to achieve self-respect, and how do we display our respect for others?

Here is a simple word that includes a profound lesson. Our parents told us, our teachers told us, and we tell everyone who will listen to us. But do we heed our own advice? Be **nice** to others. What would the world be like if there were fewer insults and more compliments?

NICE
Never
Insult
Compliment
Everyone

Think of all of the ways that you are insulted. Take the time to list some of the insults that you have received in the past day, week, month, or . . . pick a time frame. Many people probably did not realize that they were insulting you. Now, get ready for this one: Study that list. Now compose a list of similar ways that you have insulted people during that same time period. Hopefully you'll have difficulty with this challenge. Some of the insults were probably very obvious; most were probably very subtle. Do you recognize a pattern? Do we, in fact, get what we give, reap what we sow, and reflect ourselves in the mirror?

TSA
To
Show
Appreciation

NOW
Never
Overlook
Wishes

THANKS
To
Honestly
Acknowledge
Noble
Kindness
Shown

SMILE
Sure
Makes
It
Lots
Easier

KIND
Keep
It
Nice
Dear

MESSAGE
Making
Every
Statement
Significant
Allowing
Goodness to
Enter

If you don't like what you are viewing in the mirror, maybe you should put something else in that mirror. Have we just defined self-realization?

Have you noticed that people working in a store, a company, a school, or any other organization, usually display the exact level of respect exemplified by their leader? Go figure! Lee Iaccoca, while he was CEO of Chrysler, explained it this way: "The speed of the boss is the speed of the team."

We need to invest time carefully analyzing others to access their true value and strengths. What if we approached this project involving human resources much like we approach investing in our financial resources? Is there a direct correlation between investing our efforts in people and investing our money?

Many of us invest money in tax-sheltered annuities. These investments develop interest, compound, and continue to grow to enhance our financial future without being diminished by taxes. What if we use this concept for investing in our relationships with others? Can we invest in others to help create compounded interest for us? What if **TSA** stands for To Show Appreciation? Would it be possible to invest in others by simply showing them our appreciation?

Think of all the ways you can show your appreciation to people right **now**. Is there someone near you whom you could **thank** for doing something nice for you? How about a simple **smile**, a nod of your head, or a pat on the back? Is there someone to whom you could write a **kind** e-mail or text **message**? How about telephoning someone to **help** them overcome their loneliness? How about acknowledging people at work, at school, in a store, or on the street? A great gesture can be made with just one digit on one hand: Try offering a "thumbs up!"

How many times per day can we express our sincere appreciation to others? I remember the day as an administrator that I received four different thank you cards from four different people relating to four different subjects. I was stoked! We used to call these simple acts of **kindness manners**!

Would these acts of gratitude greatly overtax us; would we be gaining interest? Would it be possible, at the appropriate time, to roll our investment funds into an IRA? Remember, we have avoided being taxed, and the interest has grown, allowing our original investment to expand beyond our wildest **dreams**. We can then reap the **reward** of expanded dividends—just as we can collect from our Individual Retirement Account.

If we put our investment in an **IRA**, people would be saying things to us like, "I Really Appreciate you because . . . " Our IRA account would mature! Life would be good—especially if what we reaped didn't cost us anything to invest. Especially, if what we reaped was the magnificent **reward** of appreciation from others leading to self-respect.

A simple review of investing in respect:

TSA: To Show Appreciation
IRA: I'm Really Appreciated
REWARDS: Return of appreciation

We get what we give
We reap what we sow
We are the person in the mirror

HELP
Hurry
Everyone
Loves
Progress

KINDNESS
Keep
Intentions
Nice
De-escalate
Negative
Events'n
Situations
Swiftly

MANNERS
Make
All
Notions
Nice
Every
Response
Sincere

DREAMS
Desire
Reflects
Eventual
Achievements
Magically
Secured

IRA
I
Really
Appreciate

REWARD
Realizing
Everyone's
Work
Assures
Recognition
Deserved

How do we get started on the road to achieving self-respect? When I was in my mid-twenties, I experienced a life-changing event while attending a service in a large church in Bremerton, Washington. Many questions raced through my mind during the offertory when a long-haired hippie approached the microphone carrying a guitar. I was floored that a person with his appearance had been invited to sing a song, with guitar accompaniment, during this very traditional ceremony.

His performance of a simple popular song put many people in that large congregation into tears, including me. The song was "He Ain't Heavy; He's My Brother." The young vocalist proved to be a magnificent communicator. He brought the lyrics of the piece to life; he got the message across to us that our hearts should be full of love and respect for one another. His performance that Sunday morning ultimately changed my direction as a music educator and as a person.

My mission to perform the piece with our jazz choir began with fervor. We began rehearsing the song with the Clover Park High School Centurions. The group met two evenings a week without receiving any additional class credits. I did not receive any additional financial remuneration for my time. We volunteered to share our love and respect with one another and with our audiences. The words of the song evolved into our battle cry.

We discussed the meaning of the words in our lives and in the lives of our friends and family members. At that time, many of our friends and family were sacrificing their lives to protect our country by serving in Southeast Asia. We discussed the words from the perspective of displaying our respect for others and receiving self-respect in return. We discovered that the lessons that traveled through our hearts and souls had a much better chance of being imprinted in our minds.

Later that year the Clover Park Centurions shared that song at a statewide choral festival. The screaming standing ovation they received validated their efforts in sharing their message of love and respect for one another. The judges also validated their musical accomplishments by honoring them with the first-place trophy as members of three dozen other choirs witnessed the awards ceremony.

The group's performance began a long series of television appearances that spring, commencing with singing live on Channel Five in Seattle. It was certainly marvelous that hundreds of thousands of people could be influenced by the message being delivered through the students' musical performance via the magic of television.

To this day, it gives me immeasurable joy to visit with the members of the incredible musical **team** that brought home that first place trophy. Through their **success**, which catapulted successive groups to decades of enjoying successes, I have learned a tremendous amount about the educational process.

Do you think the vocalists remember where the contest was held? No. Do they remember winning the first place trophy? No. Do they remember their hours and hours of hard work and sacrifice to achieve their goal? No. Do they remember the concepts of hard work, sacrifice, love, and respect that have helped provide them with happy lives filled with love and self respect? You be the judge!

TEAM
Tolerance
Empowers
All
Members

SUCCESS
Seek
Understanding
Carefully
Character
Eventually
Sows
Satisfaction

CHAPTER 5

ACHIEVEMENT
<u>A</u>lways <u>C</u>ooperate; <u>H</u>onest <u>I</u>ndividuals <u>E</u>nsure <u>V</u>ictory <u>E</u>ventually; <u>M</u>ake <u>E</u>very <u>N</u>otion <u>T</u>rue

When I was a child, we lived in Port Orchard, a sleepy little village across Puget Sound from Seattle, Washington. While I was in the fifth grade at East Port Orchard Elementary School, my parents presented me with a life-changing gift. Little did I comprehend the incredible impact that a new, bright and shiny golden trumpet was going to have on my journey of discovering how to achieve life's goals!

While growing up, I had always believed that Port Orchard meant "Poor 'n Tortured" . . . until the moment that I was introduced to my new trumpet. Boy, oh boy, was I excited! I took that horn out of the case and began a rooty-tootin' away. After several weeks of practice, I thought "Mary Had a Little Lamb" sounded soooooo sweet even though my family required a very vivid imagination to recognize the tune!

When the school year began, I was so proud to carry my new little friend on the school bus to show everyone. Mr. Pickering, our bus driver, seemed to be truly excited for me, too! Things were going just great in band class; I was learning new songs and having a real blast. Yes, I was developing a feeling of **self-worth** because I finally possessed an identity based on my achievements.

Our band teacher, Mr. Ruth, employed the challenge system in class. We were placed in order of our playing abilities. If we desired a higher status in band, we formally challenged the person next to us.

SELF WORTH
Securing
Esteem
Lessens
Fear....
Working
Offers
Respect...
Triggering
Happiness

REALITIES
Realizing
Events
Accepting
Life's
Inequities
Teaches
Individuals
Everlasting
Structure

MEDIOCRITY
Muddle through
Every
Day
Insisting
On
Crummy
Results
Infamously
Topnotch to
You

If we beat that person in the challenge, we traded positions in the section. For the first time in my young life, competition became a huge driving force focused towards achievement. Many of us had dreams of becoming first chair—the very best in our section of the band!

Whoops, the **realities** of life came a knockin'! There were 12 trumpet players in our band; I was seated in the seventh chair, pretty close to the middle. That position really disappointed me. But, I wasn't yet convinced that excelling on my trumpet was worth all the hard work that Ray Anthony, a trumpet player I had seen on television, had apparently put into it.

As a fifth grader, I accepted **mediocrity**. Since then, I have discovered that you know you are a person who believes in mediocrity if you muddle through every day insisting on crummy results infamously topnotch to you!

After completing sixth grade, we headed off to Marcus Whitman Junior High School. It was a brand spankin' new school. I was so excited and totally impressed with the great building and all the "really old" students. To this day, I have vivid memories of the shirt I was wearing and the door I walked through on the very first day of school. Just like every other small seventh grader in the world, I was extremely anxious about being in such a large school with all those really big kids. Regardless of feeling very insecure, I was certainly looking forward to seeing all my buddies in band class.

Toward the end of the first week of school, Mr. Bennest, our seventh-grade band director, asked us to perform solos during class. When it was approaching my turn to play, I was hoping for the bell to end class, for a nuclear war to begin, or at the very least, for our new school to burn down. I was totally petrified! However, after several deep breaths plus a spiritual salutation, I was on the road to recovery. I was finally able to take a breath deep enough to allow me to begin tooting my horn. It's too bad you missed it; in the history of the world, I was certain "The Caisson Song" had never been performed with such musical artistry!

Just after I wowed the crowd with my stirring rendition of that goose-bump-begetting patriotic piece, this other little guy named John began wailing away on "The Little Colonel Polka." When he started playing, my jaw started for the floor. The very fortunate reality for my face was the fact that the floor wasn't too far away.

I could not believe how my entire body quivered as I heard him play. Listening to his terrific technique absolutely boggled my brain. As soon as class was over, I dragged my wilted body across the room to get in line to greet the most magnificent musician in the world—John! Little was I aware of the impact on my entire life that impromptu meeting would produce. As time progressed, John developed into my consummate role model. To this day, we are still the very best of friends.

During our discussion, I asked John how much he practiced per day. He responded, "An hour and a half." I was blown away. I hadn't practiced that much in total during the previous two months! John also mentioned that he took private music lessons once a week from Mr. Stier. I kept thinking that I would give up a very important body part or two if I

QUITTER
Quick
Understand;
Initiative
Takes
Extensive
Repetition

PROGRESS
People
Reform
Or
Garner
Refinement
Establishing
Some
Success

HOPE
Harnessing
Optimism
Produces
Empowerment

IMPROVE
Individuals
Make
Progress
Rewarding
Our
Valiant
Efforts

CANDO
Courage
Always
Necessitates
Developing
Opportunities

VISION
Very
Intense
Statement
Indicating
Objectives
Necessary

BOSS
Big
On
Securing
Success

APATHY
Awaiting
Peoples
Actions
To
Help
You

WIMP
Woe
Is
Me
Person

LAZY
Losers
Always
Zap
Ya

could play as great as John. After witnessing him perform and discovering why he was so accomplished, I felt like a ship that was sunk even before it tried to leave the dock.

I didn't want to sacrifice as much time practicing as John, nor did we have any money for private lessons. But, I didn't want to be known as a **quitter**, so I started to practice. My **progress** reminded me of what the snail said when he hopped on a turtle for a ride: "Wheeeeeee!" It's all relative. There was **hope**; I was finally starting to show that I could **improve**.

While I was in the eighth grade, John's parents made me an offer I couldn't refuse. They proposed to take me out to lunch and treat me to a hamburger, French fries, and a milk shake if I received a superior rating at solo contest. I immediately responded, "I **can do** that." Then I asked, "What's a solo contest? What does a superior rating mean?"

Many years later, I learned that Steve Ballmer, Microsoft's CEO, tells his vice president, Brad Smith, what he wants but doesn't tell him how to get there. In the Microsoft model, Brad's responsibility is very simple to understand. He establishes the business plan leading to success based on a **vision** established by his **boss**, Mr. Ballmer.

I didn't consider that a half century after I established a plan to perform at solo contest one of the richest companies in the world would be using my business model for becoming very successful. I had learned to establish a clear vision without being concerned about how to fulfill that vision. Then I developed and implemented the necessary steps to reach my goal.

I finally decided to work on improving my trumpet playing. I absolutely adored our band director Mr. Bennest; the band family was very supportive; and I especially cherished my newfound friend, John. However, as in just about every organization, many of the junior high band members could have been poster children with the word *apathy* written across their chests. They didn't care about working in band, working in other classes, or getting ahead in life.

Many of those kids had convinced themselves that they were victims of an unfair world. They spent their days aimlessly wandering about, solidifying their concept that each one of them was truly a woe-is-me person. Now that many years have passed, I have ascertained why we probably called those kids **wimps**. They displayed negative attitudes toward those of us who worked hard because they were just **lazy** losers. Have you ever considered that laziness is at the root of many peoples' negative attitudes?

I finally decided to make the commitment that I wanted to play as great as John. I really wanted the acclaim of the superior rating, but I especially yearned for that free lunch. I started to determine how to be assured that I'd receive the type of meal that had never crossed my palate. This may be very difficult to believe, but at that time there were no fast-food restaurants in our area. At that point in my life, I cannot remember ever having eaten lunch in any type of restaurant.

Let's review how the Microsoft gurus operate; first have the end in mind and then begin establishing the **plan** to fulfill the **goals**.

PLAN
Please
Learn
All
Necessities

GOALS
Greatness
Only
Awaits
Labor—
Staaaaaart

SELF WORTH
Securing
Esteem
Lessens
Fear....
Working
Offers
Respect....
Triggering
Happiness

WORK HARD
We
Only
Respect
Kindness;
Happiness
Always
Rewards
Dedication

VISION
Very
Intense
Statement
Indicating
Objectives
Necessary

GOALS
Greatness
Only
Awaits
Labor—
Staaaaaart

MODEL
Making
Observations
Determines
Every
Liking

DREAMS
Desire
Reflects
Eventual
Achievements
Magically
Secured

JOYFUL
Journey
Over
Yonder
Forget
Unnecessary
Lumps

I needed to get crackin' on preparations for the contest, so I asked our band director if he would help. Mr. Bennest, bless his heart, helped me select "Berceuse" by Godard for my solo, transcribed it, and helped me prepare it for performance. I was extremely appreciative that people were displaying their sincere interest in my musical achievements. My feelings of **self-worth** were soaring!

The next step to winning that lunch was to convince my father that I needed a specific time to practice in order to prepare for my day in the spotlight. My sales pitch evolved into a lengthy discussion regarding my desire to win a superior rating and to receive free food.

My father always got his points across in as few words as possible. That day, he forever imprinted these words on my very impressionable young mind: "You can accomplish anything within your power if you want to **work hard** enough to receive it."

If the Oprah Winfrey show had been on television at that time, I might have heard her say, "The big secret in life is that there is no big secret. Whatever your goal, you can get there if you are willing to work." If scientist Louis Pasteur had still been around, he would have said, "Let me tell you the secret that has led to achieving my goal . . . my tenacity!"

Dad and I struck a deal; he would allow me to practice every night from 8:30 until 9:00. We were building a boat, and my first responsibility was helping him with that project. Because of the upcoming salmon season, we were on a very restricted schedule to complete our boat, which we proudly named the *Able Mabel*. Little did I realize that he was training me to work hard and to be concerned with every intricate detail while we built that wonderful vessel.

We eventually completed the custom-built craft and lived aboard her at Neah Bay during the summers while we fished commercially for salmon. My fondest memories of my father are of spending our summers together braving the ocean while harvesting tons of fish.

We had established a **vision**, set **goals**, developed the business **model**, and refined the timeline. John's parents, Mr. Bennest, and my father had provided me with a succinct recipe for achieving success.

Dreams of receiving a superior rating and being honored at lunch lit a flame in my inner core that is still burning brightly today. My life has been a **joyful** journey to help thousands of people learn these principles of commitment to achieve their goals.

Did the young trumpet player discover several role models? Did he **learn** the steps necessary for achieving **success**? Did he discover that he possessed an enviable **talent** for music? Did he take a huge **risk** with his embryonic ego?

Did he really **enjoy** that mouthwatering, juicy burger with those crispy fries and that soothing chocolate shake? You betcha!

LEARN
Love
Education
Achieve
Respect
Now

SUCCESS
Seek
Understanding
Carefully;
Character
Eventually
Sows
Satisfaction

TALENT
To
Achieve,
Latent
Energy
Needs
Training

RISK
Resourceful
Individuals
Secure
Karma

ENJOY
Everyone
Now
Journey
Over
Yonder

CHAPTER 6
_____

CHOICES
Citizens Have Options Involving Commitment 'n Every Situation

You have turned to this chapter, and you read this sentence. You have made a choice. You have decided how you **want** to spend your **time**. How you choose to spend your time ultimately defines your character. If you would like expand your understanding of how to fill your life with **love** and happiness, keep reading.

One of the most memorable classes I attended at South Kitsap High School in Port Orchard was Mrs. Hilliard's contemporary world problems class. The title of the course failed to indicate the true topic of the class. Many of us felt the class would have been more appropriately labeled "Contemporary People and the Choices Available to Them."

Mrs. Hilliard wore her heart on her sleeve while she introduced us to the methods of solving our problems via the choices we would be making throughout our lives. She allowed us to openly discuss topics ranging from the incredible Elvis to the newly discovered cure for polio and decisions regarding our everyday existence. We tackled the tough issues of our society such as overpopulation, the possible inequities of the draft, and President Eisenhower's policies regarding the nuclear buildup during the Cold War.

The class discussions regarding the choices we were making in our personal lives have been forever etched in my mind. Mrs. Hilliard contended that the most difficult challenge facing us in our

WANT
Wishes
Always
Need
Time

TIME
Teaming
Insures
More
Efficiency

LOVE
Light's
On
Very
Empowering

young lives was making choices. As soon as she delivered that concept, my hand shot toward the ceiling. This sweet lady very kindly acknowledged my abhorrent appendage frantically fanning the atmosphere. I asked a very simple question in a very innocent, respectful manner. "How can our biggest problem in life involve making decisions if we are broke?" The class erupted in laughter.

I hadn't posed the question to be humorous; I was confused. After the frivolity subsided, I continued questioning her original statement. I contended that without money there isn't any need for choices because there's nothing to decide. A long, uneasy silence permeated the classroom. I had asked a very profound question that failed to solicit an immediate answer. I was considering our meager family finances as I asked this question, and I was searching for an answer. Let's look at what brought that question to my mind.

Following my parents' divorce, my mother and I were living in a very small "cracker box" rental duplex. The size of the place was the bad news; the good news was that this little rental unit was located on the shores of Long Lake near Port Orchard. I was able to spend countless hours floating around the lake searching for answers to the questions of life while casting my fishing rod.

The eight-foot boat my father helped me build was moored right in front of our duplex. What more could a young fishing fool ask for than to walk about twenty-seven feet from his front door to his boat? I rowed that tiny boat for miles and miles while pursuing the wily bass and trout that inhabited the lake's depths. This was certainly marvelous therapy for a young person who was suffering through the normal trials and tribulations of being a teenager compounded by the insecurities of a dysfunctional family.

During this time, I was struggling to earn money for college, car expenses, clothes, Friday night movies, and my fishing habit. During that period in my life, money was certainly the driving force for all my choices. It took several years for **reality** to set in. Little did I realize until decades later that I would find myself thoroughly agreeing with Mrs. Hilliard that our toughest challenge in life is making choices.

Since my high school days, I have somewhat revised Mrs. Hilliard's original statement regarding choices. For decades I have shared the following statement with thousands of people. If I could be seventeen years old again and reestablish my plans I would state it this way. "I would choose to not allow my body to become addicted to any situation or substance that would interfere with achieving a successful life."

We are living in a world that is rampant with temptations that have the potential of completely destroying our bodies, minds, and spirits. Consider the choices you have already made today. You may have even uttered some words to yourself that went something like this:

So far today, I've done all right.
I haven't gossiped.
I haven't lost my temper.
I haven't been greedy.
I haven't been grumpy.

REALITY
Recognizing
Eventualities,
Accepting
Life's
Inequities
Teaches
You

I haven't been nasty.
I haven't been selfish.
I haven't been self-indulgent.
I'm very thankful for all that.
But in a few moments,
I'm going to be getting out of bed.
From then on,
Who knows what's going to happen?

Once you decided to roll out of bed, you selected which side of the bed to get out on, what to wear, what to put in your mouth, what to allow to leave your mouth, where to park your body, when to open this book . . . the list goes on and on. Mrs. Hilliard, I totally agree with you! We make decisions every moment of every day regarding everything we do.

The choices we make help us form and ultimately define our character. That nebulous word *character* has been extremely difficult for the world to clearly define. Remember, Webster defines character as "One of the attributes and features that make up and distinguish the individual . . . The complex of mental and ethical traits marking a person, group or nation." Huh?

It might help us understand the meaning of character if we consider the correlation between Webster's definition of human character and the reason actors assume a particular role or character in a production. If you were in a play, your "character" would be based on how you act . . . notice the word *act* in the center of the word *character*? Drum roll, please: It is how we act on the choices we make that defines who we are. Do we consider all responses ethically? Do we show that we **care**? Bingo!

Mrs. Hilliard, please allow me to tell you one more time, I thoroughly agree with you. I'm not certain that you thoroughly envisioned the total breadth and depth of the statement that you made to that group of impressionable teenagers at South Kitsap High School. But you certainly have kept me thinking about it for a lifetime!

Let's take this discussion a step farther. Do you care how you act when nobody's looking? Do you notice the word *act*? *Act* is the root of the word *actions*. Do you notice the sound of the word *care* embedded in the beginning of the word *character*? Can we view human character from the perspective of how we categorize what is right and what is wrong? We make choices regarding our actions; those choices determine our character. Period.

Analyze the elements in your life and examine how those elements have evolved to establish the structure in your life. In retrospect, my reaction to Mrs. Hilliard's question was the very reason that our relationship with our instructor was so precious. She displayed her respect for our opinions by asking us to share them during class. She was certainly displaying her character. Thanks again, Mrs. Hilliard!

Throughout a lifetime of making decisions, I have referred to a set of questions posed by American clergyman Harry Emerson Fosdick. Over the years, I have altered his original statements to be somewhat more inclusive. For your benefit, please read this list several times; commit the concepts to memory. Here is Mr. Fosdick's six-point test:

CARE
Courage
Always
Resonates
Endearingly

1. Does the course of action you plan to follow seem logical and reasonable? Never mind what anyone else has to say. Does it make sense to you? If it does, it is probably right.
2. Does it pass the test of sportsmanship? In other words, if everyone followed this same course of action, would the results be beneficial for all?
3. Where will your plan of action lead? How will it affect others? What will it do to you?
4. Will you think well of yourself when you look back at what you have done?
5. Try to separate yourself from the situation. Pretend, for one moment, it is a situation being faced by a person you admire the most. Ask yourself, how would that person handle it?
6. Hold up the final decision to the glaring light of publicity. Would you want your family and friends to know what you have done? The decisions we make in the hope that no one will find out are usually wrong.

Did you notice that those six statements explain how to determine the difference between right and wrong? The overriding question in your life has probably revolved around that issue. Tons and tons of material have been written and gazillions of hours have been spent exploring this issue. The monumental question of your life has probably been, how do I decide what is right and wrong for me? Gulp! Let's attempt to simplify this question.

Take a moment and think about the beliefs of ten people you know fairly well. If you were to discuss their opinions of what is right or wrong on any given subject (yes, any given subject), you can be certain that you would hear many similar views. But for the most part, you would hear ten different perspectives.

Suppose we use the love of music as an example for this test. As everyone is aware, there is a myriad of different genres, styles, forms, combinations of performers, famous artists, topics of songs, etc. Think about the number of recordings available to you on television, on radio, online, and in stores.

Would your ten friends all line up their top one hundred favorites in exactly the same order? Not a snowball's chance in a hotspot! We all choose tunes based on our personal likes and dislikes and how we feel at the moment. It sounds just like the way we make other decisions in life, doesn't it?

We just made an assumption. We assumed that everyone likes to listen to music. Wrong! As an example, right now, I can't stand to listen to music! After more than half a century of being totally consumed with making music as an instrumentalist, vocalist, teacher, conductor, clinician, adjudicator, and administrator, I am currently refusing to be actively involved. As I write this, I feel a huge part of my existence has escaped from my body, mind, and spirit. I am dying inside. It absolutely kills me to listen to music. **Music** magnifies our understandings of the meaning of life. Right now, I do not want to be reminded of those joys that are missing from my life.

The joys of being involved in creating music with people who also have a **passion** for this process are beyond explanation. Will I change my opinion about music? You're darn right, when I finish this project and have the time to again be involved as an adjudicator and guest conductor. But

MUSIC
Mankind's
Ultimate
Study
In
Creation

PASSION
People
Always
Seek
Success
If
Opportunity's
Noble

RULES
Regulating
Us
Leads
Everyone to
Success

LAW
Learn
Allowable
Ways

FREEDOM
Forget
Restrictions
Enjoy
Every
Days's
Opportunistic
Moments

US
Understand
Self

for now I have made a choice to attempt to affect the most people in the best possible way, and I'm sticking to it.

Let's start thinking about those ten friends of yours again. How do they decide what's right and wrong regarding their values, morals, and ethics? You probably agree that those ten people have ten different sets of self-imposed **rules** of life. How do we learn and establish those rules of right and wrong to govern our existence?

Rules govern our lives for a reason. Imagine you're traveling down the highway. Whether you are driving or riding in the car, you are governed by lots and lots of rules. If it's dark, are your lights on? Do you have your seatbelt properly secured? Has your vehicle been properly licensed? Does the driver possess a valid driver's license? To license the vehicle, you may have had to pass an emissions test. Are you proceeding at the speed limit, not too fast and not too slow? Are you traveling on the correct side of the road? You had better know the laws of the country you are in!

If you break a rule, that is called breaking the **law**. If you break the law, your **freedom** has been judged to have been imposing upon the rights of others. There are consequences for people who fail to abide by the rules. There are tow trucks, body shops, handcuffs, jails, emergency rooms, hospitals, morgues, and cemeteries. Yes, if we are not responsible in our own actions, there are consequences. How do we decide what's right and wrong for **us**?

How do we decide our rules of life? We establish our own set of rules based on a multitude of considerations. What process do we employ to help us decide between right and wrong?

Please consider this process. Everyone's life is a sequence of thousands and thousands of events. We call these events experiences. Our minds establish a method for categorizing and storing information regarding these events. This storage method, of course, is called memory. You're saying "I know that."

Let's analyze how our memory affects what it stores and how it stores the information to enable us to develop our concepts of right and wrong. First of all, we flat out forget most of the information that enters our mind via our senses. We especially fail to remember the things that cause us emotional and physical discomfort; that process is called repression. Repression is usually a good thing; there is a reason we put our garbage in a can and it goes off to the dump! It usually stays there—hopefully buried very deep. Some of our garbage is recycled; be aware of your recycled products. Those products might reappear in the form of a suitcase. We call that baggage! How much recycled baggage do you want to carry around with you? Do you have so many suitcases piled around you that you have trouble wading through them? It's your choice!

Do we, in fact, categorize right and wrong in our brains? Sure we do. When we experience something that we consider the right thing to do, our thought process works something like this: I respect the person who said it; they convinced me that it's correct; it's going to be filed in the "that's-right file." When we experience something that we think is wrong, we say something like this: The person who

CONSCIENCE
Categorizing
Our
Notions,
Selecting
Choices,
Influences
Everyone's
Noticeable
Character
Eventually

said that convinced me that it's wrong; I'm adding to my current knowledge base on that subject; I'm convinced that's not the correct thing to do; that's wrong. It's going to be placed over here in the "that's-wrong file." What if we store those files in a folder and we label that folder our **conscience**? One more time: What if we store those files in a folder and we label that folder our conscience? That folder is then stored in the most magnificent computer ever invented: our mind.

What are we implying when we use expressions such as "my grandmother displayed such a kind spirit when . . . " or "the team had such a fantastic spirit when . . . " or "I thought of my fishing experiences with my father when I decided that . . . ," etc.

Consider the word *experience* for a moment. Say it out loud. Do you hear the root of the word *spirit* in the center of word *experience*? What if we view our experiences in life as the *spirit* of others being shared with us? Our recollections, memories, lessons, and experiences of situations and individuals are overflowing in our existences with their spirits. Hold that thought!

In the research for this project, I've spent many, many hours asking people what bothers them the most about other people. The earth would need to give many trees for me to list all of the criticisms! However, the word that has surfaced time and time again during this study has been *hypocrisy*, which basically means that someone failed to deliver on a promise. You're thinking of other words aren't you—words such as *lie*, *distrust*, *deceit*, *dishonest*, and *disgrace*. The list goes on and on, I agree. However, *hypocrisy* seems to be the cesspool for all the rest.

Here comes a "**what if**." What if we try to avoid using the term *walk the talk*? In other words, what if we try to avoid always saying what we are going to do? Such statements can very easily evolve into promises. As soon as we use the word *promise* are we facing the possibility of hypocrisy right square in the eye? What if we simply employ the spirits from our life experiences to guide our actions? What if this compilation of spirits that we have filed away in our folders in this colossal computer called our mind could be labeled our conscience? What if we simply display our beliefs by using this compilation of experiences called our wits? Then our **wits** can be "Walking In The Spirit." Making use of our memories can be defined as **wisdom**, or "Walking In Spirit Directing Our Memories."

I have two questions for you right now. Do you see how concepts of right and wrong are developed? Do we ever need to be concerned about being hypocritical in the future if we simply **wow** people by "Walking Our Words?"

Just a minute; there is a huge responsibility with this approach. Would you agree that if we are to decide what is right and wrong we are obligated to filter what comes into our computer? Quick, let's install the virus protection and the firewalls in our minds. Let's make it very simple: garbage in, garbage out or goodness in, goodness out. You decide!

Do you remember John, the trumpet player I met in the seventh grade? Remember, he became my role model. Let's go back and take a look at how the conscience of a junior high school student was developed. Let's analyze how my mind was imprinted with John's family values, both good and bad.

WHAT IF
We're
Happiest
Always
Thinking,
Initiating
Fantasies

WITS
Walking
In
The
Spirit

WISDOM
Walk
In
Spirit
Directing
Our
Memories

WOW
Walk
Our
Words

POLICE
Politeness
Only
Lasts
If
Citizens
Empathize

ARREST
A
Required
Reservation
Employing
Self-discipline
Training

ABUSE
All
Beings
Underestimate
Some
Eventualities

EVIL
Every
Vicious
Individual
Loses

Everyone knows that our lives ideally revolve around doing everything that we do in moderation. Remember our example of the speed limit on the highway? If you go too fast or too slow you will be faced with paying the consequences; breaking the rules of the road can result in receiving a ticket from the **police**. If things really go bad, the police may even **arrest** you!

During our junior and senior high school years, John's house became my second home. His family was a perfect example of some of the television shows of the time. Walking in the door of John's home was like turning on the TV and watching *Leave It to Beaver*, *Ozzie and Harriet*, or *Father Knows Best*.

John and his two younger siblings were all overachievers; to say the least, they enjoyed loads of well-deserved success in their activities. They were highly respected by their teachers and peers and had great grades. You name it; they were the perfect example of an all-American family. However, little did I realize the level of **abuse** that was festering in this seemingly beautiful household.

John's parents really enjoyed their beer. As the years passed, their level of alcoholic beverage consumption dramatically increased. Their demeanors took an abrupt nosedive when they drank; they always become very negative and extremely argumentative. They seemed to explode over the most trivial situations. After a few years, my desire to visit their home diminished. Seeing them in their drunken stupors just tore my heart out. The family I had grown to love and admire so deeply was rapidly deteriorating because they were exemplifying that the **abuse** of alcohol leads to **evil**.

As the years passed, I avoided visiting John's parents. Seeing their lives taking such a downward spiral was becoming intolerable. One day, a tragic realization unfolded while I was shopping in a small grocery store near their home. An elderly man was standing in line in front of me. His long graying, greasy hair nearly reached his waist, and his beard was nearly as long as his hair. His filthy fingernails curled like daggers, and his clothes were so dirty and grimy that they stuck to his flesh. He reeked of cigarettes in addition to the odor of cheap wine; the stench of his body was absolutely overwhelming.

When it was his turn, he plopped his box of beer and bottle of wine on the counter and fumbled through his pockets to come up with enough crumpled cash to give the clerk. He then picked up his bounty and struggled out the door to share his treasure with his wife. The clerk said, "See ya later, Mr. . . . ." My heart sank right through the floor. You guessed it. The loving couple who had basically adopted me as a child had now officially adopted a new love that had transformed their entire lives—**alcohol**.

In spite of my disappointment in his parents, John and I remained very close friends. As the years passed, rumors regarding their overindulgence surfaced often. Frequent encounters with law enforcement officers and regular trips to the hospital became normal for this couple. John's mom's habit of neglecting food necessitated multiple trips to the emergency room to combat her malnutrition. Alcohol had become her food of choice.

Late one night, I received a phone call from John. He started his normal pleasant chatter, as

ALCOHOL
Always
Limit
Consumption,
Often
Hinders
Our
Lives

though he was trying to mask an event. I knew something horrible had happened. I asked him a simple question. Which one? He said, "Mom."

In an effort to console him, I asked the typical questions. When did she pass away? John said, "I don't know." Where was she found? John replied, "In her bed." Where was your dad? John said, "He was in the house with her." I phrased the question differently. Do you have any idea when she died? John collapsed into tears and sputtered out, "The county coroner thought she had been dead for at least eight days." Why didn't your dad tell you sooner? "For over a week, Dad thought Mom was just sleeping; he was too drunk to tell that she was dead."

The following Saturday, at her funeral, the pastor didn't waste any words. With the family's permission, he explained how her dependence on alcohol had killed her while crippling her husband and emotionally maiming their family.

The very next day, my emotions transcended from the depths of depression to the heights of exultation. A very unique celebration occurred early that morning at our church; it was the absolute antithesis of what had happened with John's family. Just before the eight o'clock service began, about fifty people ranging in age from babes in arms to a very elderly couple triumphantly proceeded up the center aisle and were seated in the front pews.

I had never witnessed such a happy, exuberant, joyous entourage in our church. At the beginning of the service, our pastor turned to the congregation and proudly announced, "Let's join the children, grandchildren, and great-grandchildren of Mr. and

Mrs. Murphy in honoring them on this very, very special day in their lives—their sixtieth wedding anniversary!" I was deluged with tears as I thought, "If only . . . "

John's Dad's severe nerve damage, a result of decades of alcohol abuse, led to his death shortly after John's mom's funeral—once again proving that alcohol kills! Their beautiful children were no longer burdened with the acute problems of chronic alcohol abuse. Life-long anguish? You decide. It's your choice.

CHAPTER 7

TRUST
Thoroughly Relying Upon Someone's Tenacity

While I was the choir director at Stadium High School in Tacoma, Washington, a very sad event occurred. Joey, one of our outstanding choir students, became ill. The day he stopped by the school to gather his possessions, he told me how perplexed he was because his doctors were having difficulty diagnosing his illness. But he valiantly said, "Don't worry, Mr. B, I'll get well and be back singing real soon." I responded "Joey, your **health** should be your main concern; don't worry about us, but you know that we'll do everything and anything we can for you." Little did I realize the gravity of the statement I had made to Joey. It would ultimately measure the depth of the word *trust.*

A few days after our discussion, Joey lapsed into a coma. He was transported by helicopter to the University of Washington Medical Center and placed on life support. As soon as I heard the horrible news, I raced off to visit him in Seattle. His family's **hope** for his survival was very dim. The next day, I took David and Marcus, his two closest friends, to visit him. As you would expect, they were completely devastated. On our drive back to Tacoma, we discussed how we could **help** Joey's family during this incredibly difficult time.

On Friday night of that week we opened the musical *Oklahoma.* After the show, we were informed of the sad news that Joey had passed away earlier that evening. The next morning, I called his

HEALTH
Hopefully
Everyone
Accesses
Life's
Trip
Happily

HOPE
Harnessing
Optimism
Produces
Empowerment

HELP
Hurry
Everyone
Loves
Progress

PLAN
Please
Learn
All
Necessities

mother to share my heartfelt condolences, and through our tears we pondered several questions.

I asked Joey's mom if she had any plans for a service for Joey. She explained that everything had happened so fast that she had absolutely no plans. I asked, "Will you trust me to take care of the plans for you? What if I call you back later today and see if you approve of my ideas?" She responded that she would wait for my call and was extremely appreciative of my efforts.

Fortunately, I knew the staff of a large church near the high school. Through a series of phone calls, the staff and I organized a **plan** for Joey's final service. I explained the plan to his mom; she concurred, and we started the wheels in motion.

During that time, the staff at Stadium High School was the most loving group of people imaginable. Their love permeated the atmosphere of the entire school community and was in a big part due to the influence of Stadium's very highly respected principal, Mr. Shain. He was the epitome of how a true leader leads by influence. Because he ruled by example, he didn't need many rules. The kids loved him, the staff loved him, and the community loved him.

The following Friday at 12:30 in the afternoon, Mr. Shain announced to the students and faculty that they were excused from classes to attend Joey's service. Nearly the entire high-school population began a procession to the church to say their final farewells, filling the sanctuary to capacity. By excusing the students, Mr. Shain had displayed his respect for Joey and his love for the entire school community.

For all seventy members of our Chanticleer **Choir** to be in the line of sight for my conducting, we needed to be on opposite sides of the church. Consequently, the choir was positioned in the balcony on one side of the sanctuary, and I was in the balcony on the opposite side. Joey's body was lying in his casket between us at the front of the church. Most of the students in the choir had never attended a funeral, so in preparation for the service we had spent most of our class time that week discussing the tragic loss of their classmate. Throughout our discussions, we tried to imagine how they would **feel** when it came time for them to share their music.

During the service, testimonials were given while images of Joey's life were displayed on the wall in the front of the church. As we had anticipated, this experience sent most of the singers collapsing in grief. So many tissues and handkerchiefs were being used that the group looked as though they had been struck by a snowstorm. As I looked across the expanse of the church, I was thinking that during my entire career this was absolutely the most unrealistic challenge I had ever requested students to fulfill.

We had discussed this exact scenario earlier in the week. We knew that we would need to concentrate on the message when it was time to share our music with Joey's family and friends. Anything less than a magnificent performance would rob everyone, including ourselves, of the magical healing powers of the **music**. We needed to think only about sharing our gifts; any other thoughts would be **selfish** and would doom our efforts to failure.

CHOIR
Caring
Hearts
Offer
Inspired
Relationships

FEEL
Faith
Eventually
Elevates
Love

MUSIC
Mankind's
Ultimate
Study
In
Creation

SELFISH
Sure
Everyone
Loves
Fulfilling
Individual
Success'n
Happiness

The time arrived to display our level of trust in one another. Marcus, Joey's close friend, started the solo that begins the choir arrangement of "Ain't Got Time to Die." His magnificent booming baritone voice resonated throughout the church. The choir entered with the same passion and conviction that Marcus exemplified; I was absolutely astounded. The next selection was a hauntingly beautiful setting of "Shenandoah" arranged by James Erb. At the conclusion of the songs, the vocalists' tears began flowing again as they collapsed back into their pews.

As I was being seated, Mrs. Long, who was seated behind me, leaned forward and whispered, "Bruce, I just witnessed a miracle!" I replied "Mrs. Long, I just had the most profound choral conducting experience of my life because I trusted those magnificent kids in that sensational choir!"

What if others are relying on us, and we don't pull through? What if we say, "I won't take the initiative; somebody else can do it?" What if we don't help because we don't want to **risk** becoming involved? How should others feel about us if we always say, "I coulda, shoulda, woulda?" What if we think we understand a situation but it turns out that we are incorrect?

I spent seven summers in southeast Alaska fishing commercially for salmon. One summer, an experience afforded our crew an opportunity to display how we could be trusted. The boat I was working on had been constructed in Hydaberg, Alaska; hence, it was named the *Hyda Boy*. A tall, lanky fellow nicknamed Spider had previously worked on the *Hyda Boy* but had become the skipper of his

RISK
Resourceful
Individuals
Secure
Karma

own craft named the *Bull Moose*. The crews of the two boats were constant companions. Our boats traveled together, we fished together, and we spent our days off pursuing adventures together. The crew members of both boats placed total trust in one another, guarding against any unforeseen eventualities.

During an extended weekend, we decided to depart from the quaint little village of Hoonah and cruise to a lodge that had recently been constructed on the shores of Glacier Bay. During our voyage, Bill, the owner of the *Hyda Boy*, was at the helm while I was busily preparing dinner in the galley. During the trip, I made several trips to the top of the wheelhouse to retrieve supplies for the "super stew" I was concocting. I always glanced back to make certain our friends were still proceeding in our wake. Just after we turned from Icy Straights to venture into Glacier Bay, I noticed the *Bull Moose* was no longer behind us. I mentioned my observation to Bill, and we joked that maybe they had just rolled over and sunk. Then we discussed that they had planned to stop to gather Dungeness crabs and to fish for halibut. We knew they would have called us on the radio if they had needed our assistance.

A few minutes later, we arrived at Glacier Bay Lodge. As I was completing dinner preparations, the crew departed to view the gorgeous new lodge. About an hour later, George, one of our crew members, ran to tell me that Spider was standing on the dock wrapped in a blanket. I immediately bolted up the ladder and found Spider, totally disheveled, soaked from head to toe. I peered down and saw that three of his crew members were also wrapped in blankets. The *Bull Moose* had departed Hoonah with six men.

The boat had sunk right behind us. The two crew members who were sleeping below deck went down with the boat to a watery grave. The four crew members who were topside scrambled overboard as the boat rolled over and sank. Sport fishermen in a passing boat had rescued the survivors and brought them to rejoin us—the crew they thought they could trust.

You probably agree that trusting people is exemplified by saying something like, "I have the highest respect for the people who are always there for me." I have heard this statement from hundreds of people describing what they respect the most about others. Many times friends who will be there for us are like stars: You know they are always there; you just don't see them all of the time. Like stars, in time of darkness, our friends can shine a light to help us on our journey through difficult times.

One of the previous situations depicted friends successfully displaying trust. The other situation displayed trust being usurped by a horrible accident. What can we do to ensure a level of trust with people we do not know?

Our dog, Skipper, and I recently returned from prefishing a bass tournament in Eastern Washington. We were fishing out of our high-tech bass boat that has copious amounts of locking storage for all of our fishing tackle. We had spent two days interviewing other fisherman, and we were able to "pattern the fish" by experimenting with a variety of techniques in different spots. Through our efforts we determined that the bass were beginning their days by feeding very early in the morning near the water's surface.

At the end of our second day of fishing, I neatly organized eight of my very expensive bass rods on the front deck of our boat so we would be ready for the next day's predawn action. We parked in a beautiful spot in a campground with a locking gate to sleep overnight in our truck camper with the boat on the trailer, attached to the truck. I trusted the security of the campground; I trusted my guard dog's keen senses; and I trusted the people near us.

The following morning we stepped out of the camper at about 4:00 a.m. and discovered that the rods and tackle boxes that were so neatly positioned in the bow of the boat just feet from where we were sleeping had disappeared!

Had I trusted myself to understand all of the security issues of the campground? Had I trusted Skipper to bark if someone came near our equipment? Had I trusted in the honesty of others not to **steal** our expensive equipment? Can I trust the **police** to recover the stolen booty? Can I trust our insurance company to cover the entire loss? Can I trust what comes out of my mouth considering how I might overreact to others during this time of **stress**?

How could I have avoided this dilemma that has put a screeching halt to our plans of competing in the upcoming bass tournament? Duh! I could have spent five minutes locking up the equipment in the storage areas of my boat. Who should we always be able to unequivocally trust? Let me explain it this way: Since this incident have I spent a considerable amount of time questioning the person in the mirror? Trust me!

STEAL
Sometimes
Trusting
Everyone
Activates
Loss

POLICE
Politeness
Only
Lasts
If
Citizens
Empathize

STRESS
Some
Think
Redirecting
Energy
Saves
Sanity

CHAPTER 8

EMPOWERMENT
Everyone Manages Productive Opportunities With Each
Response, Mending Every Negative Thought

The key to self empowerment and empowering others is to understand needs and to help fulfill those needs in a positive manner. Did we just define quality teaching?

After interviewing many, many people, I have discovered that one element right near the top of everyone's list of desires is for others to listen to their opinions. Do you listen to the people you associate with? Do they listen to you? Is there a reason we have two ears and only one mouth? It shouldn't require a calculator to determine the percentage of time each of these portions of our anatomy should be utilized.

Dick Vermeil has spent most his life as a very successful football coach. During his first two years with the St. Louis Rams the team won a total of nine games, a horrible record. Curt Warner, the Rams quarterback has described the players' relationship with Vermeil during that time period as very strained. Curt explained that Dick had certain coaching methods, and it was the players' responsibility to learn and to abide by those methods. Needless to say, the won–loss record indicated that things were not going very well for Mr. Vermeil and the Rams. His autocratic methods were obviously not producing the results that anyone desired.

At the beginning of Vermeil's third season with the Rams, the team members began to stage a mutiny. They held a team meeting and decided to

CATALYST
Change
Always
Takes
A
Leader
You
Should
Try

LOVE
Light's
On
Very
Empowering

MONEY
Move
Over
Negativism
Enter
Yes-man

FEEL
Faith
Eventually
Elevates
Love

ART
Always
Representing
Truth

rebel against his psychological tactics and his torturous workout regime. After Vermeil learned of the meeting, in an effort to preserve the franchise and his job, he decided to take a totally different tack with the team.

The quarterback, Curt Warner, explained that the turnaround for the Rams came when Dick asked the team, "What do you think?" Vermeil became a **catalyst**, and the players became empowered. The Rams won the Super Bowl that season, and Curt Warner was selected as the Most Valuable Player of the game. Case closed!

Let's take a look at the actions and reactions of the loves we have in our lives to help us understand the meaning and importance of empowerment from a personal perspective. How can we tell if we really **love** somebody or something? Isn't it ironic how we talk about our love of sports, music, nature, parents, family, neighbors, hobbies, and the list goes on and on? What do we mean by saying that we love something?

After I retired from working in public schools, the state offered retirees a financial incentive to return to work that was difficult to ignore; they offered the highest possible step on the salary scale in addition to letting us collect our monthly retirement benefits. In other words, by being a "retire, rehire person" we were able to increase our salary by sixty per cent. Math has never been my forte, but it was easy to figure this one out! Hopefully, we love what we do, but it does take **money** to pay the bills.

Consequently, I decided to accept the position as choir director at Steilacoom High School and Pioneer Middle School. These small schools were only about one-third of the school population I was accustomed to serving. However, because of the tremendous administrative interest and support, choir enrollment soon skyrocketed. It was a fantastic opportunity to work with kids from grades six through twelve in a wonderful community nestled on the shores of Puget Sound just three miles from our home.

As it worked out, in the twilight of my forty-year career, many of the students in Steilacoom and I had been together for six years. Talk about being in love with a group of kids! During the spring of that final year, the students in the Steilacoom High School Pinnacle Choir were discussing their perceptions of their last performance. They were thrilled with the audience's reaction at their concert. Of course, we loved the performance because we loved making music with one another. Toward the end of our discussion, I asked a very simple, straightforward question, "Are we involved in this and the other events in our lives simply because of how those activities make us **feel**?"

The choir students had learned to open their hearts and souls to the fundamentals of learning how to sing and craft their choral **art**. At performances, they were able to share their sincere feelings via the magnificent medium of **music**.

In summing up our discussion I asked, "Is the bottom line of our efforts as a choir, and in life receiving **joys** to replenish our **soul** and then sharing those **joys** with others? Can we conclude that it really boils down to how our **actions** make us feel? The students voiced their agreement with my concept of empowerment. We had come to totally accept the **truth** and **beauty** of human relationships,

MUSIC
Mankind's
Ultimate
Study
In
Creation

JOYS
Just
Open
Your
Soul

SOUL
Source
Of
Unconditional
Love

JOYS
Just
Offer
Your
Spirit

ACTIONS
Allowing
Change
Towards
Improvement
Offers
Needed
Success

TRUTH
To
Respectfully
Uncover
The
Honesty

BEAUTY
Beloved
Experiences
Always
Useful
To
You

GREAT
Golden
Rule
Elevates
All
Teams

IMPROVE
Individuals
Make
Progress
Rewarding
Our
Valiant
Efforts

TEACH
Teaming
Eventually
Activates
Correct
Habits

empowering ourselves to enable us to empower others with our love.

True empowerment is much more than Henry Ford's providing his factory workers with tools and the first assembly-line concepts so they could build Model Ts. True empowerment is teaching others while bearing in mind that our primary student is our self.

In the middle of my career, I spent nearly a decade serving as a school district administrator. By observing **great** teachers, I learned a multitude of important lessons regarding effective teaching. My greatest challenge, which I truly enjoyed, was helping teachers learn how to **improve** their teaching techniques. Most of my colleagues loved their jobs, and as expected, some needed help recognizing the positive aspects of their positions.

One of my responsibilities as music supervisor was to help the music staff become more effective in sharing their love of music with students. One day, I received an urgent phone call from a secondary principal. The principal said, "Bruce, get over here and **teach** your music teacher to control his classes, or I'm going to **fire** him." My mission was certainly made very clear; it's great to have challenges in life! What if we view tough situations as challenges rather than merely problems? That viewpoint will challenge us to reach our **goals**, not just to **worry** about our problems. It does absolutely no good to worry about something we have little control over. Is this another example of thinking from a **positive** perspective?

I contacted the teacher without explaining the seriousness of the situation concerning his future employment. Was this an example of how total honesty is not always the best policy? We established a **plan** for classroom observations and discussions following each observation.

Everyone should have such a wonderful opportunity to analyze human behavior with a room chock-full of adolescents. How do we define the term *eye opener*? While I was sitting in the back of the room taking notes, several issues surfaced. It was very noisy because the kids were entertaining themselves as the teacher was attempting to instruct. The students who were trying to listen couldn't hear the teacher. Students seemed to be using a multitude of methods to circumvent what they were being asked to do. It was a perpetual battle between the teacher and the students over who was going to be directing the energy in the room. My, oh my, there was certainly lots of energy in that room! We just needed to discover a method of redirecting and focusing all that **pep**.

During quality observations, I always follow the same format. It goes like this: "You said . . . ; they responded . . . . Here are some things you might consider next time. . . . " After a time, I realized the instructor had established a definite pattern of delivery. His statements were always framed the same way. He would say, "I want you to . . . "

Our one-on-one coaching sessions revolved around the challenge of changing his focus from "I want" to *their* wants. It's really simple, isn't it? This person was attempting to sell music to kids. In his autobiography, Lee Iaccoca, the former CEO of Chrysler, states that if you want to sell anything to anybody, you have to approach it from the perspective of their wants and needs, not yours.

FIRE
Free
Individuals
Real
Effectively

GOALS
Goodness
Only
Awaits
Labor—
Start

WORRY
Wickedness
Only
Result'n
Resentment
Y'know

POSITIVE
Please
Offer
Sincere
Insights
To
Instill
Values
Effectively

PLAN
Please
Learn
All
Necessities

PEP
Positive
Energy
People

ACCEPT
All
Circumstances
Can
Eventually
Produce
Truth

IDEA
Inspiration
Deserves
Everyone's
Attention

The atmosphere of the classroom turned around immediately when the instructor started approaching the art of teaching from the students' perspective via the game of discovery. The students' minds became engaged when he began teaching by challenging them with questions. As expected, they started answering those questions and they began asking the teacher more questions. Keep in mind that a boomerang that doesn't come back is called a stick! Does a successful leader need to rule with a club?

The music students became focused on fulfilling their personal desires of achieving a quality musical experience. The noise level diminished; the number of discipline problems dwindled; and the teacher received an outstanding evaluation and a contract for the following year. Why? The person in the front of the room had learned a critical aspect of quality human interaction: empowerment!

Remember, the act of teaching involves persuading yourself and others to "**accept** the value of an **idea** or product." Does this mean that teaching is really an act of salesmanship? When people ask me what I did for a living, I tell them I was a music salesman. I have experienced a wonderful life convincing thousands of people to embrace the love of music to provide them with joy and comfort for a lifetime.

Is everyone a teacher? Yes. Whether we are a student in the fifth grade, working on an assembly line, cooking in a restaurant, developing real estate, laboring at a computer, flying an airplane, or working at any other occupation, we are learning with a teacher involved. That teacher might be standing in front of us in a formal setting, or more often than not, our number-one teacher wears our clothing. You got it; our primary teacher is our self. Hopefully, we are perpetually experiencing positive empowerment!

How do we define the steps of empowerment; is it sales or is it teaching? Is it possible to view empowerment as sales and sales as teaching? Consider viewing them as one and the same. I have delineated the following steps involved in teaching as the "Seven C's of **Sales**":

1. Courage
2. Connect
3. Challenge
4. Channel
5. Check
6. Confidence
7. Celebrate

1. COURAGE

Many people have the **courage** to sell themselves and their **ideas**, but some people are too **shy** to **try**. If you currently lack the courage, you'll need to make a conscious effort to develop that part of your personality. It takes a great deal of courage to impose your will on others. You must be sold on the fact that your concept or product is of value to the consumer. If that is not true, you might be involved in a **lie**.

Here's a case in point. I once was a very skinny vacuum cleaner salesman; I didn't make enough money to eat on a regular basis! There was a simple reason for my lack of success. I was not convinced that my customers would die unless they

SALES
Sincere
Attitudes
Launch
Everyone
Successfully

COURAGE
Carefully
Observing
Underlying
Risks
Allows
Goals to
Evolve

IDEA
Inspiration
Deserves
Everyone's
Attention

SHY
Sure
Hurts
You

TRY
To
Respect
Yourself

LIE
Losers
Intentionally
Exaggerate

bought the brand of vacuum cleaner I lugged from door to door. I lacked the courage to lie to them.

I was earning money to pay for college; however, peddling this very expensive vacuum cleaner also provided a very valuable learning experience. The canned sales pitch gave me great practice in public speaking and in teaching. Remember: teaching is sales, and sales is teaching. Not only did I show prospects how to use the equipment, I attempted to persuade them that they couldn't live very much longer on this earth without it. Convincing people of that wasn't always **easy**.

EASY
Everybody
Always
Says
Yes

The sales presentation always concluded with a demonstration of sucking the gunk out of the prospective customer's mattress with that powerful machine. I showed the folks the amount of dead skin and disgusting debris they were wallowing in as they slept. Then I pointed out that there was a good possibility they would die from a multitude of mysterious illnesses unless they immediately signed a contract to buy this fantastic machine that would eradicate the gross gunk in their midst. The filth was truly disgusting; however, it certainly wasn't life threatening. I was caught up in a cycle of delivering hogwash to close a sale. I hated lying. I was not sold on the value of the product. I didn't have the courage—nor did I want—to lie, so I quit.

2. CONNECT

My wife accuses me of having way too much extra time on my tongue. She knows what words will fall out of my mouth when I have the chance to visit with a stranger. In an effort to get to know someone, I look them straight in the eye and I phrase the questions just like this: "Hi, my name's Bruce. What's your name? Where are you from? Where did you grow up? Where did you (do you) go to school?"

The persons' eyes automatically light up, and they freely begin talking about themselves. Some additional questions pop up, like, "What do you do during the daytime?" This question is a catch-all inquiry; it is much safer than asking "where do you work?" The person might be a student or a stay-at-home mom or dad, retired, or unemployed. Then I ask, "What do you do when you aren't working (going to school, etc.)?" If it hasn't been mentioned yet, I ask them about their favorite **hobby**. These questions will definitely indicate that you are interested in them. Oh, the things we can learn from others by asking simple questions!

3. CHALLENGE

We need to be aware that all of us search for challenges to give us a sense of fulfillment. Psychologist Clayton Alderfer included this concept in his ERG theory (existence, relationships, and growth). He espouses that every human being is motivated by fulfilling three basic desires:

- Existence essentials like water, food, and shelter
- Relationships with other humans
- Growth in personal development and challenges

In simper terms, we humans by nature are hunters and gatherers. We innately respond to

HOBBY
Healthy
Options
Bring
Back
Youth

BORED
Bring
On
Remembrances
Every
Day

BORED
Bring
On
Recreation
Every
Day

BORED
Bring
On
Relationships
Every
Day

FUN
Forget
Unnecessary
Nonsense

ENJOY
Everyone
Now
Journey
Over
Yonder

MEMORIES
Most
Events
Make
Our
Recollections
Youthful

HOPE
Harnessing
Optimism
Produces
Empowerment

DESIRE
Does
Everyone
Strive
In
Reaching
Excellence

DREAMS
Desire
Reflects
Eventual
Achievements
Magically
Secured

MIND
Magical
Insights
Now
Develop

challenges that have helped us survive throughout millennia. The desires to survive, to enjoy companionship, and to be productive are simply in our genes. Does it follow that these concepts are at the root of all of our competitions to fulfill these desires? Do we always need to be the "winner" in all of our endeavors? Do we view our lives from the perspective of a sporting event mentality? Do we always need to label a winner and a loser in everything that we engage in? Can that attitude cause us immeasurable heartache throughout our lives?

The downside of wanting to be productive is the reality of becoming bored when we are not productive. The number-one complaint students have about schools, workers have about their jobs, and people cite for failed relationships is not being challenged. Simply put, they are **bored, bored, bored**. A recipe is available to help counteract boredom; it is called "keep challenging ourselves." That is certainly easier said than done.

How do we turn all our miniscule tasks into **fun** experiences? How do we **enjoy** times that by themselves are not exciting? We go on trips—lots of trips! We have imaginations; we have **memories**; we have hobbies; and we have **hopes, desires**, and **dreams** to pursue. Our **minds** can be full of those thoughts during times of boredom. We certainly need to re-create ourselves when we have the opportunity. Remember, *re-create* is the root of the word *recreation*. We need to do things when we aren't involved in boring tasks, so we have something to think about during those times of boredom. I sure caught a lot of fish during that class that bored me in high school!

The founder of Disney Studios, Walt Disney, said, "When you're curious, you find lots of interesting things to do." The late Jim Croce wrote and performed a tune titled "Time in a Bottle" that truly encapsulated Walt Disney's concept. A line in that song is the quintessential statement about remaining intrigued with our lives: "But there never seems to be enough time to do the things you want to do once you find them."

While I was traveling in Europe one summer directing a choir comprised of students from throughout the northwestern United States, Barbara Williams, one of the group chaperones, summed it up this way: "It's great for these kids to have these experiences; it will give them something to think about when they are home working at their boring jobs, doing dishes, and changing diapers." Thank you, Mrs. Williams!

4. CHANNEL

We need to develop our **plan** and then establish the steps required to reach our **goals**. Here's how we apply this concept. While I was a senior in high school, I had set a goal to become a music teacher. That goal required **money**. That goal required a **job**. I was **broke**, so I needed to channel my efforts to secure the funds to pay for college. I explained my financial plight to a friend of mine named Ron; he agreed to help me learn to pick salal and huckleberry brush. Brush picking is a skilled labor that involves gathering evergreens to sell to floral companies. I began as a very ineffective brush picker; it took a lot of instruction and practice to become proficient. Ron introduced me to his friend, Norman is

PLAN
Please
Learn
All
Necessities

GOALS
Goodness
Only
Awaits
Labor—
Start

MONEY
Move
Over
Negativism
Enter
Yes-man

JOB
Just
Over
Broke

BROKE
Bountiful
Revenue
Only
Keeps
Escaping

CONFIDENCE
Changing
Our
Negative
Fears
Invites
Delightful
Experiences
Never
Considered
Easy

LEARN
Love
Education
Achieve
Respect
Now

EMPOWER
Everyone
Makes
Pertinent
Observations
With
Every
Response

CONFIDENCE
Changing
Our
Negative
Fears
Invites
Delightful
Experiences
Never
Considered
Easy

a fellow who had a great deal of **confidence** that he could help me **learn** how to pick brush.

Norman took me to his father's 2000-acre brush lease and taught me how to pick brush. His kindness helped pave the way for me to fund my college education. He channeled my efforts to **empower** me with the skills to earn money to pay for school. Remember the statement that you get what you give? I am forever deeply indebted to Norman and his family. I have expressed my gratitude in many ways. I am proud to say that I introduced him to a close high-school friend of mine from Port Orchard, and they have had a very loving marriage with many children and grandchildren!

5. CHECK

Dr. Donald Goetschius, a professor of education at Central Washington University, said, "Pay close attention to the barometers in the room." He pointed out that we should always watch the facial expressions and the body language of the people we are talking with. Steve Ballmer of Microsoft also suggests that eye-to-eye contact is still the best method of judging responses from others. My career was spent standing in front of large choirs studying how a stimulus affects the response. I am convinced that all of our actions have reactions; we just need to make certain we pay close attention to them!

6. CONFIDENCE

One year, the students in the Synergy Jazz Choir at Stadium High School had a discussion regarding building the **confidence** of all group members.

They decided to establish a very honorable goal of enabling each of the twenty-four vocalists in the group to sing a solo in public. It was certainly a struggle; however, all of the singers, plus the members of the combo, received their exclusive moment in the spotlight. All the members of that compassionate **team** were thrilled!

I explained to the musicians that Miss Nicholson, my college speech professor, espoused that it is possible to present any topic to anyone, in any situation, without **fear**, if you are convinced of the value of the message. Our mission in singing solos was exercising the **passion** to get the **message** across. By concentrating on the message in the words, the vocalists were able to overcome their anxieties and fears to empower themselves with the confidence to succeed in their performances.

When I attended graduate school, I spent a very long time working on my master's thesis. Finally, the time came to conclude my degree by completing an oral examination. I had written a book titled *Developing the High School Vocal Jazz Ensemble*, and I wanted to get through the final exams, get out of school, and get on with teaching. Just thinking about the oral exam made me about as nervous as an alley cat on a hot tin roof, three miles from dirt, having to visit the restroom real bad!

The exam consisted of being grilled by two music professors and a professor from the department of education. The butterflies in my belly fell into formation when a simple thought finally crossed my mind. An air of serenity consumed me as soon as I realized that nobody in that group knew as much about the subject of vocal jazz as I did. I

TEAM
Tolerance
Empowers
All
Members

FEAR
Freezes
Every
Action....
Reconsider

PASSION
People
Always
Seek
Success
If
Opportunity's
Noble

MESSAGE
Making
Every
Statement
Significant
Allowing
Goodness to
Enter

HOPE
Harnessing
Optimism
Produces
Empowerment

DREAMS
Desire
Reflects
Eventual
Achievements
Magically
Secured

PRIDE
People
Respect
Individuals
Delivering
Excellence

HUMBLE
Hurry
Understand
Me
Bragging
Loses
Everything

decided to enter that two-hour talk-a-thon from the perspective of teaching my instructors about the joys of vocal jazz. It worked! We had a great time. They loved what they learned, and I received my master of education degree! But more than that, I learned to have confidence in my product's value and to display the passion to get my message across.

7. CELEBRATE

Would you agree that improvement is a great thing to celebrate? Confucius said, "It's alright to take small steps; just don't stop." In other words, perpetual improvement is the key to successful empowerment. We need to celebrate each step of improvement. Do you think the builders of the great pyramids, the Panama Canal, or the great cathedrals of the world celebrated each small step leading to the completion of their final product? Let's hope so, because many of the craftspeople who started those projects didn't live long enough to celebrate the final completion. We should always celebrate the progress in the process, with the **hope** of celebrating the final product.

The happiness you experience in fulfilling a **dream** certainly needs to be celebrated, with restraint. When you make that sale, win that game, score well on that test, collect that trophy, or procure that long-sought-after possession, keep one factor in mind: the PH factor. It is certainly appropriate to have pride in an accomplishment, but remember that **pride** needs to be balanced with remaining **humble**. Always approach your celebrations while considering the feelings of those who were not as fortunate.

It's all well and good when things go according to the Seven Cs, but what happens when we stumble over others while pursuing our **dreams**? Might an act of contrition be in order? Do we respect people who share their sincere forgiveness?

Is forgiveness simply the act of overcoming negative events by putting them in a positive light without seeking retribution? Do we understand that relationships are much more precious than the trivial matters that can destroy them? Can you recall relationships with acquaintances of yours that have ended over insignificant disagreements? You probably remember the friendship's ending, but can you remember the exact reason for it?

For seven summers I fished commercially for salmon in Alaska. We spent two months living and working in extremely cramped quarters with a crew of five or six people. Can you even begin to imagine the challenges we faced in maintaining healthy relationships in that compressed environment? If we became upset, could we hop in our car and drive away, go to our room, sulk off to the far end of the house, or go for a walk around the neighborhood? No. We learned a very safe, guaranteed place to escape. That place was labeled "forgiveness."

At times, the "heat of battle" was very intense. We were in direct competition with the boats fishing the same area for the available fish. The faster and more efficiently we worked, the more money we made. It was truly a **team** effort because we received a share of the **profits**. We learned to tolerate one another's level of intensity to succeed. Even though we were very driven, we learned to say things like, "I'm sorry, I didn't need to **yell** at you."

DREAMS
Desire
Reflects
Eventual
Achievements
Magically
Secured

TEAM
Tolerance
Empowers
All
Members

PROFIT
Providing
Revenue
Opportunities
Fulfills
Individual
Tasks
Successfully

YELL
You
Eventually
Lose
Love

SORRY
Success
Often
Requires
Rescinding
Yourself

FORGIVE
Freeing
Our
Resentment
Garners
Increased
Value
Everytime

"I'm **sorry**, I shouldn't have pulled on that net web so hard with your fingers entwined." Or, "I'm sorry I was being a jerk!" We learned to seek forgiveness because the ocean water in Alaska is really cold. It's deep too!

Randy Milholland, an American humorist said, "Sometimes the measure of friendship isn't your ability to not harm but your capacity to **forgive** the things done to you and ask forgiveness for your own mistakes."

One of the immense rewards of being involved in music education has been sharing the joys of music with others. My mountain-top experiences have been when others have been inspired to fall in love with making their own music, a testament to true empowerment in action.

In December 2002 three of the Steilacoom High School choirs visited Wah He Lut Indian School on the banks of the Nisqually River near Olympia, Washington. It is a beautiful new school featuring an entrance that is a replica of an Indian long house.

It was a dark, dreary, rainy, wintry day when we arrived for our performance, after which we were to be the school's guests for lunch. Our choirs presented a sensational array of holiday songs that were loads of fun to sing and extremely entertaining for the audience.

At the conclusion of our performance, we asked the students at Wah He Lut if they would like to perform for us. A group of kindergartners was absolutely bubbling over with enthusiasm to oblige. The example of empowerment that transpired that day will be with me until I enter my grave.

We were thrilled to watch the group of little

tykes excitedly assemble on the stage to perform some of their traditional Native American songs. We were spellbound as we witnessed them pour their hearts into their performance. We sincerely acknowledged their outstanding efforts with a huge ovation. As the students were exuberantly exiting the stage, one little boy just couldn't contain himself any longer. He thrust his fist to the sky in a victory celebration as he blurted out, "I just love to sing! Look!" He pointed to the massive window where a patch of blue sky had just appeared. "Our singing made the sun come out!"

Young man, thank you so much for displaying the possibilities available to the people of the world if we, too, can ultimately believe in the strength of true empowerment!

CHAPTER 9

RELATIONSHIPS
Realizing Every Love Allows Truth In Our Normal Situations, Helping Individuals Proclaim Self-Worth

During commencement addresses, you would expect that presidents of major universities would stress the quality of their institution's educational process. Not so when Dr. William Gerbeding spoke several years ago at the University of Washington in Seattle. Instead of offering a laundry list of the university's strengths he spoke to the **hearts** of everyone in attendance. His commencement speech very effectively defined the essence of what it means to be human. Dr. Gerbeding challenged the graduates to remember these three **facts**:

HEART
Help
Everyone
Achieve
Respect
Today

- You will forget almost everything you learned before you were twenty-one.
- Keep the shower curtain inside your tub.
- Who you take with you is more important than where you go.

FACT
Finding
Actual
Circumstances
True

If you were one of those graduates sitting in Husky Stadium wearing a flowing purple graduation gown and a flat little mortar board on your head, you were probably saying to yourself, "Let's get this thing over with. I'm tired of flippin' burgers; I just want to be flippin' my tassel to the opposite side of my mortar board and getting on with my life."

Then, as though a bolt of lightening hit, you would have thought, "Did that guy just say what I thought he said? I just spent the better part of a king's ransom to go to school here, and now is he telling me that I'm going to forget almost everything I learned? I wonder if that means I get my money back?"

Do you have any idea what Dr. Gerbeding meant about forgetting almost everything? Do you remember the hours and hours you studied for tests to prove how effectively you memorized the facts? Do you recall how you ingested the material, spewed it out onto the test paper, and then immediately forgot most of the answers? That's what he was referring to: the small stuff, the nonsensical stuff, the minute details, the inconsequential facts.

Do you know why Dr. Gerbeding won't be offering you a refund? Because by memorizing and spewing those facts onto that paper you were practicing. Yes, you were practicing and, hopefully, perfecting the most important facet of the educational process. You were learning how to **learn**.

When we are learning something new, we need to be very careful to learn the information correctly in the very beginning. Many of us believe that repeating something just three times will imprint the learned response in our minds and bodies. As an example, if students took sheet music home and learned it on their own, I hoped they would learn it absolutely correctly because if they learned anything in the piece incorrectly, it would be very difficult if not impossible to correct. The imprinting process sometimes called body memory or muscle memory takes over, and the newly learned material is nearly permanent. Be extremely careful while developing your learning skills; remember that im-

LEARN
Love
Education
Achieve
Respect
Now

properly learned information and skills will be very difficult if not impossible to change! After several years of studying this phenomenon, I developed an axiom that states, "Practicing imperfection makes imperfection perfect!"

When Dr. Gerbeding said, "Keep the shower curtain inside the tub," you may have thought of the traditional commencement celebration. Your mind may have overflowed with images of those flat little mortar boards soaring into the sky and showering down on you and on your fellow graduates. Wroooooooooong!

By keeping the shower curtain inside your tub, he meant that you should be **responsible** for your own actions. Dr. Gerbeding was reminding you that before you say or do anything you should make certain to consider the consequences of your **actions**. Is your path of action going to hurt you or someone else? Remember just about everything that's **bad** starts off to be **fun**. There is usually a very fine line separating those two concepts. One test for displaying outstanding personal character is being able to recognize and appropriately respond to the information on both sides of that fine line.

You probably liked the part of his speech about taking a shower. Taking a shower makes a person feel really good! Just remember, several responsibilities are involved when you take a shower. You need to wear the proper outfit, in this case your birthday suit (which is usually fairly easy to locate), step into the enclosure, and turn on the water. The water needs to be adjusted to a comfortable temperature and to the correct amount of pressure and aimed at you.

RESPONSIBLE
Reconsidering
Every
Situation
Prevents
Occasional
Negative
Standards
Influencing
Behavior
Leading to
Extremes

ACTIONS
Allowing
Change
Towards
Improvement
Offers
Needed
Success

BAD
Bullies
Always
Destroy

FUN
Forget
Unnecessary
Nonsense

STRESS
Some
Think
Redirecting
Energy
Saves
Sanity

You grab the soap and lather up. You sing and scrub and scrub and sing and sing and scrub and scrub and sing . . . you are in the zone. You keep scrubbing away until you're squeaky clean. Because your curtain is inside the tub, all the waste water goes down the drain. You finish up, dry off, get dressed, and go about your daily routine. Can we structure our lives to be as joyous and as satisfying as that feel-good-all-over shower?

To help us explore that question, let's study a poem by Robert Frost titled "The Pasture." See if you can discover how this poem describes the process we need to follow to discover comfort, rid ourselves of **stress**, and find purpose in our lives. As you read this poem, see if you can discover how important love and caring are in everlasting relationships? See if you can discover what the ultimate goal of life should be.

The Pasture

I'm going out to clean the pasture spring;
I'll only stop to rake the leaves away
(And wait to watch the water clear, I may):
I shan't be gone long.—You come too.

I'm going out to fetch the little calf
That's standing by the mother. It's so young
It totters when she licks it with her tongue.
I shan't be gone long.—You come too.

OK, you're probably thinking, "Huh?" Let me shine some light to help you interpret this poem.

What if we view the pasture spring as describing how our lives flow? What if we consider that raking the leaves away is the manner in which we can remove our undesirable traits and habits? You are probably aware of those traits and habits; they are the elements in your life that are bothering you and infringing on the relationships with yourself and with those around you.

Can we practice the patience to develop relationships and to ultimately realize the main ingredient of personal happiness? The mother's relationship with the calf sums it up; their display of caring and love says it all. Like the little calf, what level of comfort would you feel in your life if you knew that your relationships would be nurtured forever?

Like most people, I worked at a wide variety of jobs to survive throughout my college years. One of my toughest jobs was as a hod carrier for a bricklayer. The job consisted of mixing the mud (cement) and distributing the building materials for the laborers who were laying the bricks. It was truly back-breaking work; however, it was much easier on my back than on my mind.

It was tough enough being a greenhorn, but my **boss**, Ralph, seemed to be impossible to satisfy. In his opinion, everything I tried was wrong; he could have been the poster boy for disrespect and negativism. He certainly taught me the meaning of the word **demand**. Even though I have had lots of bosses as a logger, a salesperson, an educator, a commercial fisherman, and countless other jobs, Ralph won the prize for being the crudest, rudest, most negative, sarcastic person with absolutely the foulest mouth of anyone I have ever worked with.

BOSS
Big
On
Securing
Success

DEMAND
Do
Everything
Management
Asks
No
Discussion

One day during our lunch break, as I was devouring my Spam sandwich, I complimented Ralph on how kindly his wife, Rosemary, treated everyone. Then I began asking this huge hulk of a man some questions about her—the typical questions such as, "When did you meet Rosemary? How long have you been married? What do you like most about her?"

I was absolutely floored by the way he responded. As soon as Ralph began talking about Rosemary, he turned into a gigantic cream puff. His eyes lit up, and a smile as big as all outdoors spread across his face. I was then treated to a magnificent soliloquy beyond compare!

When his love story neared completion, I was eager to ask him some questions about my own embryonic love life. A wonderful young lady and I were in the midst of trying to determine the depth of the love in our relationship. I was finally able to work up the nerve to ask Ralph a simple question. His explanation has done more to clarify the true meaning of love than all of my experiences since then.

I very innocently asked, "Ralph, how can you tell when you really love someone?" Ralph set down his can of soda and gazed across Hood Canal toward the Olympic Mountains. After a long silence, he looked back at me, his eyes welling with tears, and he replied "Bruce, you'll know . . . because when that person walks into your life, the lights will turn on . . . and you'll have the feeling that you can accomplish absolutely anything in this world . . . because you . . . will be . . . in **love**."

How do we begin relationships? Our high-tech world has certainly created many avenues for

LOVE
Light's
On
Very
Empowering

meeting new people. Regardless of how we meet others, the fundamentals governing relationships always remain the same. The number of fish in the sea makes no difference if they are not interested in what we have to offer to attract them.

Do you remember the seventh-grade-band story I related earlier? Do you remember when I raced across the music room to compliment John on his trumpet performance? That was a perfect example of the ancient adage, "If you want to find a friend, be a friend." How did I display my friendship to John? How did I display my friendship to Ralph, my bricklaying boss?

It is so simple . . . I complimented them. No insults were involved; I was **nice**. It was very easy being nice to John. I simply mirrored his actions towards me. If I had mirrored Ralph's actions, I would have lowered myself to his level. I would have been delivering insults to him; I chose not to do that.

NICE
Never
Insult
Compliment
Everyone

I worked with great diligence to display kindness towards Ralph; I killed him with instant kindness, the **kwik** principle. My efforts garnered great dividends. Sure I earned money, but the real value was much greater than financial. I learned positive things, and I learned negative things. I learned what to include and what not to include in my personality. The poet, philosopher, and artist Kahlil Gibran once wrote, "I have learned silence from the talkative, tolerance from the intolerant and kindness from the unkind. I should not be ungrateful to those teachers."

KWIK
Kill
With
Instant
Kindness

While preparing students for a vocal solo contest a few years ago, a young student and I were rehearsing a piece of music titled "None, But the Lonely Heart." This very intelligent musician was not

LONELY
Love
Only
Needs
Escape;
Life
Yearns

LIFE
Love
Is
For
Everyone

BELONG
Beautiful
Encounters
Let
Opportunities
Now
Grow

NEEDED
Notice
Everyone's
Esteem
Develop
Each
Day

singing with the yearning tone I was striving for her to exhibit. I looked at her and said, "Anita, this song is about being **lonely**; you sing as though you've never been lonely." Anita looked back at me and said, "I'm sorry, Mr. B; I've never been lonely." Oh, the innocence of youth, compounded by the danger of making assumptions. Needless to say, we began the search for a different solo for her to perform.

Then Anita explained why she had made that statement. She told me about her wonderful family, her community, and her school activities. She explained the level of responsibility she assumed in caring for her younger siblings. Then she told me about the joy that she received from her **life**. She truly possessed the elements in life that lead to personal happiness. We discussed three important ingredients in her life that brought her so much joy. She had a sense of belonging, she felt needed, and she felt loved. Since then, I have studied those elements in great detail. I am now thoroughly convinced that we all strive to **belong**, to be **needed**, and to be loved.

You might be saying to yourself, "I'm not sure that's so important." Bear with me a moment. I want to tell you about a movie titled *Cipher in the Snow*. You may know that the word *cipher* means "zero."

The movie is said to be a reenactment of a true story. It begins with a school bus loaded with junior-high-age children traveling down a country lane blanketed with snow. A young boy walks up to the bus driver and asks to get off the bus. He steps out into the snow, collapses, and dies. The autopsy reveals that his heart had simply stopped.

The remainder of the movie chronicles the boy's school experience. During the investigation, school officials discovered that he had attended schools in that town all his life, but he was not involved in any school activities. They were unable to find a teacher who knew anything about him other than his grades. Many students were interviewed, and nobody knew anything about him except his name.

One day I showed this movie to a high school choir. After the presentation, the students slowly began meandering back to the music room. Kathy sought me out and shared some of her perceptions of the movie in a very somber tone. I encouraged her to continue elaborating on her story. She went on to explain that she knew the story we had just witnessed was true. She very softly said, "I know it is true; my five-year-old brother recently died from exactly the same cause. His doctor told us that he probably didn't feel that he belonged on this earth and his heart simply stopped." Through her tears, she later related the horrible **tragedy** to the entire class.

On a recent cold, dark morning Skipper, our little bouncy bichon frise puppy, and I were driving off for our morning walk to his favorite place in the world: the park. **Freedom** to be on my own time schedule is definitely a benefit of retirement, even though I sure miss the kids! We were traveling behind a school bus loaded with high-school-age students. We stopped behind the bus as a group of students was boarding their big yellow taxi. Memories of my bus-riding experience raced through my mind as I watched the students file on the bus. I was wondering how the three elements

TRAGEDY
Terrible
Results
Accentuate
Grief
Everyone
Deliriously
Yearns

FREEDOM
Forget
Restrictions
Enjoy
Every
Delightful
Opportunistic
Moment

SMILE
Sure
Makes
It
Lots
Easier

COMFORT
Consolation
Often
Means
Forgetting
Our
Realities
Today

of our human-needs concept would be fulfilled on that crowded bus. This was the students' first test of the day regarding their feelings of belonging, being needed, and being loved.

A not-so-very-happy young woman was leading the file of new riders to the rear of the bus, searching for a seat. I could see her very clearly; it was dark outside and the lights were on inside the bus. An instant smile spread across her face, and she sat down. I surreptitiously said to Skipper, "Sure Makes It Lots Easier!" Much to my astonishment, I had just delivered the acronym for **smile** by describing how it signals fulfillment in our lives. Needless to say, I was much more excited than Skipper; his eyes were focused on the nearby park. He didn't seem to be overly impressed with my efforts in helping the world be a happier place!

There seem to be four major elements that determine the success of any relationship. These four elements refer to relationships with anyone in any situation. You can simply change some of the details to help them fit the relationships you are assessing, whether they are with coworkers, classmates, neighbors, friends, family members, or others. For this example, let's use romantic relationships. Here are the elements:

- **Comfort**
- Goals
- Mystery
- Timing

The first ingredient for successful relationships is an extraordinarily high level of *comfort*. You can list many traits that fall into this category. There must be a high level of respect, trust, honesty, understanding, tolerance, fun, kindness, charity, manners, values, ethics, humor, unselfishness, forgiveness, and the list goes on. What traits would you add to this list?

The second ingredient is *goals*. Do you support your loved one's goals; do they support yours? This issue is fairly straightforward . . . until it comes to details like money and family. How do you prioritize your spending, saving, and investing? How do you get along with each other's friends and family? Do any undesirable habits impede the relationship? Do you wish to have children? How do you prioritize what's important in your life? Where do you want to work? Which hobbies do you wish to pursue? Where do you want to live? Where do you want to vacation? How do you celebrate life's joys?

Is there a level of *mystery* in the relationship? Are you perpetually attempting to get to know the other person even better? Do you keep trying to unlock the magic of their being? Are both of you always developing as human beings by exercising your curiosity through becoming lifelong learners? By continuing to improve as a person and developing intellectually, you become a perpetual source of inspiration to each other. These elements certainly fall under the old adage that opposites attract.

Finally, is the *timing* correct? Do these elements of your personalities have an opportunity to be discovered while the two of you are available for an active relationship with each other?

To view a wider screen of the intricacies of love, let's study how a Nobel Peace Prize recipient, Mother Teresa, describes the importance of love in relationships in her book titled *Meditations from a Simple Path*:

> Love has no meaning if it isn't shared.
> Love has to be put into action.
> You have to love without expectation,
> To do something for love itself,
> not for what you may receive.
> If you expect something in return,
> then it isn't love,
> because true love
> is loving without
> conditions and expectations.

These thoughts should all be balanced with some sage advice I heard from the pulpit: "True love is much more than a feeling; it is a commitment." Does the commitment in your relationship remain even after the intensity of the emotion begins to fade?

Can we expect to have "perfect" relationships? Certainly! If we are perfect to begin with! Would you agree that trying to attain perfection is what keeps us interested in greeting tomorrow? One of my high-school classmates summed it up this way: "If life is always perfect here on earth, would there be a need for a heaven?"

How should we view our day-to-day relationships with everyone in our lives? For several years, I walked through the Pioneer Middle School cafeteria on the way to teaching my final class of the day. About the time I arrived, the custodian, Mr. Pine, was usually finishing up his duties cleaning the lunch room. I always made it a point to exchange some pleasantry with him. It might have been something regarding the news of the day, a fishing story, a new joke, a story of a school event—just anything to help acknowledge him and his hard work.

One Monday afternoon, I shook his hand and thanked him for doing such a great job of cleaning the sidewalks after the previous day's snowstorm. Yes, he had spent several hours of his time on Sunday shoveling snow to ensure the safety of the students and staff. He had once again been displaying his kindness to us.

Later that same school year, I visited an acquaintance of mine, Mr. Hamilton, who worked in a neighboring school district. I reminded him that every time I hit one of the "arrow" keys on the computer, I thought of him and how he taught me how to use "the magic carpet ride" on that Apple IIe computer years ago. I again thanked him for the kindness he had shared with me on his own time.

Why do I tell you these stories? Those incidents were the last times I saw these people. Shortly after I saw Mr. Pine, the custodian, he had an apparent heart attack and was found passed away in a storage area at the school. My friend Mr. Hamilton fell out of his small boat and drowned a few weeks after our last conversation.

What would our relationships with others be like if we treated each of our daily encounters as though it would be the last time we could see that person? One more time: What would our relationships with others be like if we treated each one of our daily encounters as though it would be the last time we could see that person? I can guarantee you one thing. All relationships end; there will be a last time we will see everyone we know. What would relationships be like if we treated everyone as though it would be our last chance to share joy and kindness with them?

The Stadium High School Chanticleer Choir offered their music at the funeral of a choir member's sister who had passed away in her mid-twenties. She was survived by her husband and three very young children. Near the conclusion of the service her husband stood at her open casket, embracing a bouquet of roses as he lamented over his lost love's affection for roses and his eternal love for her. As you might expect it was an excruciatingly sad experience for everyone in attendance. He presented the roses to her in a heart wrenching display of affection, proclaimed his final farewell, and the service precipitated to a close. The choir members were totally debilitated. A choir member named Josh tried to console Denise by saying, "Denise quit crying." Through her flood of tears she blurted out, "Leave me alone, I want to **cry**." She was inconsolably immersed in the beauty of the grieving process; she had made it crystal clear to Josh that she wanted to cherish every moment of that eloquent experience.

You would probably agree that bidding a final farewell to others is the most difficult part of living. Would it be comforting if you could learn to **accept** the grieving process as a journey, not just the final destination? Could you try graciously greeting grief, appreciating grief, and celebrating grief? What if you try viewing **grief** as a joyful sojourn to illuminate your view of the memories of your loved ones? What if you ultimately allow those magnificent memories

CRY
Caring
Reveals
You

ACCEPT
All
Circumstances
Can
Eventually
Produce
Truth

GRIEF
Granting
Respect,
Inspiring
Everlasting
Friendships

to resonate in the expanse of your **soul**? Losing others helps us to comprehend and quantify the value in our existing relationships, eventually filling the void left in our lives by nourishing and further developing our current relationships with others.

SOUL
Source
Of
Unconditional
Love

What if you try celebrating your grief from the perspective of the value of the love that you have shared with the departed? The depth of loss that we experience is in direct correlation to the heights of love that we celebrated for those we are grieving. The deeper our love, the deeper our loss, the deeper we grieve. Loss is to love as wind is to fire: it extinguishes the insignificant, and it enkindles the magnificent.

The puzzle of life is never as simple to comprehend and neatly order as the picture puzzle that we excitedly dump out of a box and gleefully arrange on a table. The puzzle on the table has a very definite sense of closure, but this puzzle we call life?

You may recall that Christopher Reeve played the title role in the movie *Superman*. A few years after he appeared in the starring role, he fell from his horse and was permanently paralyzed. Shortly after his premature death, his wife Dana Reeve was diagnosed with terminal cancer. While she was deeply grieving for her late husband and facing her own mortality, she said, "Life isn't fair, so you'd better stop expecting it to be." Dana Reeve passed away shortly after issuing that courageous epitaph.

Would it be comforting if we could view our bodies as flowers of the fields and our existence as the ever changing seasons? Just like flowers, we know and hopefully can learn to accept that our bodies experience growth, maturity, decline, and departure. Let's study a poem composed by Christina Rossetti (1830–1894):

Bitter for Sweet

Summer is gone with all its roses,
Its sun and perfume and sweet flowers,
Summer is gone, summer is gone,
    summer is gone
And even autumn closes
Yea autumn's chilly self is going;
And winter comes, which is yet colder;
Winter comes; winter comes, winter,
    winter, winter
Each day the hoar-frost waxes bolder;
Winter, winter, going.
And the last buds,
    the last buds cease blowing.

What if we view our bodies as though they are like the roses in the poem? Just like rose bushes, we are different sizes, shapes, ages, and colors, and we have different expected life spans. What if we view the peak experiences in our lives as the blossoms radiating from the rose bush in full fragrant splendor? The more memorable experiences we accumulate, the more blossoms we produce throughout our lives. Some people's lives are perpetually filled with beautiful blossoms; others may have only a few blossoms or none. Rose bushes, like people, have varying numbers of thorns; people, like rose buses, also have varying numbers of less than desirable traits that can be offensive.

Hopefully the flower's life span, like ours, will not be diminished by natural occurrences or by **abuse**. If

ABUSE
All
Beings
Underestimate
Some
Eventualities

the roses are transplanted, recovering from the journey may prove very difficult if not impossible. When autumn arrives, the petals of the blossoms wilt, let go, and begin daintily twirling, drifting, and dancing on the chilly breeze to gently descend to their resting place on the earth. The leaves on the trees celebrate the flowers' passing by glowing with the golden autumn hues that signal the impending advent of winter. It's a glorious sight; Mother Nature is inviting life back to join her on the earth.

Winter arrives signaled by an aging frost that blankets and preserves the beautiful setting; the future buds are deeply encapsulated in the plant, patiently awaiting Mother Nature's signal for emergence in the spring. Life's journey on earth has reached an end. Just like the flowers, we, too, are invited to reunite with Mother Earth. Hopefully the seeds of our spirits and the spirits of our lost loves will be preserved and will have the opportunity to resonate through the souls of others as they in turn blossom.

Am I able to heed my own advice in overcoming the despair of losing loved ones? I **try**! Do I still crumble into crying bouts thinking about losing my parents a quarter of a century ago? I am proud to say yes! What does this signify about the depth of my love for both of them?

TRY
To
Respect
Yourself

May I suggest three very basic steps to pursue in all relationships to help us learn to experience a more satisfying life and, hopefully, to help us achieve everlasting peace of mind:

We learn to Live.
We learn to Love.
We learn to Let Go.

CHAPTER 10

INSPIRE
Individuals Need Support Philosophically In Reaching Expectations

When I was very young, Mr. and Mrs. Ibsen from Port Orchard invited our family to attend their church with them. It was never clear to me why our parents did not join us. But they did make sure that all four of us children rode to church with the Ibsen family, no ifs, ands, or buts about it. For several years, my siblings, and I knew exactly where we would be every Sunday morning.

To remain in good favor with our hosts, we had to abide by several basic rules. We always wore our Sunday best (talk about a term that's lost its meaning); we walked to the Ibsen's house and arrived on time; we attended Sunday school; and then we fully participated in the very long church service.

We have many fond memories of attending that gorgeous little church in downtown Port Orchard. The Sunday-school teacher, one of the Ibsen daughters, instructed us in lessons regarding **respect**, **love**, **caring**, **hope**, and **faith**. She implanted in our impressionable young minds the seeds of understanding what it means to be **blessed**. She also encouraged us to display our newfound inspiration by singing. Boy, did we like that part!

At the church services, I looked forward to sitting as close as humanly possible to Mr. Ibsen. My, oh my, did I **try** to sing as loud as he was singing. He amazed me! Not only did he possess a heavenly sounding singing voice; he even closed his hymnal before the end of the songs. He had those songs memorized!

RESPECT
Recognizing
Everyone's
Strengths
Produces
Exceptional
Caring
Teams

LOVE
Light's
On
Very
Empowering

CARING
Citizens
Always
Respond with
Integrity
Not
Greed

HOPE
Harnessing
Optimism
Produces
Empowerment

FAITH
Forget
All
Insecurities;
Trust
Hope

BLESSED
Bountiful
Love
Endures
Scorn 'n
Sadness
Enters the
Deity

TRY
To
Respect
Yourself

MUSIC
Mankind's
Ultimate
Study
In
Creation

KIND
Keep
It
Nice
Dear

Mr. Ibsen was truly my role model. He was so deeply respectful of all his friends, his family, and his church. But, most of all, he was a great singer. He seemed to sum up all the loves of his life when he sang. He was absolutely astounding, and I wanted to be just like him!

Legend has it that I had the opportunity to prove my singing prowess to the congregation. My sisters, who are both older than me, have related the story—many times—of my inspirational vocal performance at one of the church services. Dr. Phil, the television personality, points out in his book "Self Matters". . .**music** is a very important force in our lives. I set out to prove his statement true even before he was born!

Apparently little Bruce refused to sing in the children's choir (maybe his agent wouldn't let him). However, he did accept an offer to perform a solo for the congregation. Can you imagine how the tears must have tumbled when a cute little four-year-old poured his heart and soul into expressing his newfound faith by singing "Jesus Loves Me?"

To this day, one of the great unsolved mysteries in my life is why our parents withdrew their support for our church attendance with our **kind** neighbors. I am certain that Mom and Dad never fully realized the impact that spiritual experience had on four little wandering **souls**.

As a very young child, I did not comprehend or fully appreciate the manifestations of our church experience. However, after many years of college and forty years of serving as a professional educator, I feel that I am beginning to recognize its impact on our lives. The children in our family had serendipitously discovered a refuge that fulfilled the three most essential ingredients in our lives. When we attended that church, we found that we belonged, we were needed, and we were loved. The older I get, the more that I am convinced that these realizations of self-worth are at the core of human existence.

The **realities** of life came crashing down around us when our parents told us that they were getting a divorce. None of us was aware that event was even on the horizon. In retrospect, our folks had never gotten along. As expected, their constant unhappiness with their relationship overflowed into their interactions with us. Our once secure home had become a very negative, often hostile, battleground that wasn't healthy for anyone.

This once loving husband and wife had sadly reached the point of no return with their marriage. All four of us children experienced tremendous **guilt**, assuming that the responsibility of raising four kids on a shoestring budget in a very small house finally drove both of them insane. As time went by, how we yearned for our happy home and the safe haven of the church from our past.

The words to the song that I performed in that church as a four-year-old kept cycling through my mind. Surprise! Only when **prayer** again became an important part of my life did I rediscover the **power** of those wonderful feelings of security I had experienced as a little tyke.

Years later, while I was fishing for steelhead trout way down in a very deep, dangerous canyon in Washington's upper Skokomish River, an **idea** slammed into my skull. "Mother Nature has created so much beauty; she's planned and created all of

SOUL
Source
Of
Unconditional
Love

REALITIES
Realizing
Events
Accepting
Life's
Inequities
Teaches
Individuals
Everlasting
Structure

GUILT
Giving
Up
Inequities
Leaves
Trust

PRAYER
Powerful
Resources
Await
Your
Every
Request

POWER
People
Only
Want
Elevated
Respect

IDEA
Inspiration
Deserves
Everyone's
Attention

PLAN
Please
Learn
All
Necessities

MEANING
Making
Every
Action
Naturally
Include
Noble
Goals

RULES
Regulating
Us
Leads
Everyone to
Success

LONELY
Love
Only
Needs
Escape;
Life
Yearns

these breathtaking mountains and this gorgeous singing river. Maybe I should start searching for part of that **plan** and renew my journey to discover the **meaning** and **rules** of life." I certainly didn't desire to spend my life in the downward spiral of negativism and unhappiness that my parents had experienced.

Witnessing the implosion of my parents' twenty-six-year marriage proved to be extremely devastating to a very impressionable, emotionally fragile teen. I yearned to experience a happy life. Being **lonely** certainly wasn't going to be an option as far as I was concerned. I needed lots of help in understanding how to be **happy**. My search to discover the rules of **life** had commenced.

My friend of several years, John, the magnificent trumpet player, listened to my yearning to find security in my life. He invited me to attend his church. I loved the way I felt comforted after attending the church service. I also visited the church I had enjoyed as a child. John's church seemed to fit my needs **best**. His church seemed to be very serious about addressing the struggles of everyday life. I attended the church's introductory classes and joined John's congregation during my senior year of high school.

After attending Olympic Community College in Bremerton, Washington, for two years, I enrolled at Central Washington University in Ellensburg. While singing in a church choir in Ellensburg, I met two sisters who were also singing in the choir. These wonderful young ladies took it upon themselves to informally adopt me into their very large, loving family.

John visited me in Ellensburg for a weekend,

and we took this opportunity to invite these lovely ladies out to dinner. John immediately fell in love; I'm proud to say that I was the best man at their wedding. They have had a wonderful life together that has been blessed with several wonderful children and a house full of grandchildren.

John inspired me to become deeply involved in music. He also inspired me to become deeply involved in his church. His future wife appeared while I was pursuing the inspirations he had introduced into my life. His efforts to inspire me were rewarded with the most magnificent gift imaginable, the woman of his dreams. And they have lived happily ever after!

HAPPY
Have
All the
Peace 'n
Pleasure
Ya want

LIFE
Love
Is
For
Everyone

BEST
Beautiful
Endeavors
Seem
Terrific

CHAPTER 11

SELF-WORTH
Securing Esteem Lessens Fear; Working Offers Respect, Triggering Happiness

We are currently waging a battle against terrorism throughout the world; wars and perpetual conflicts are erupting in bloodshed on a daily basis. Will the inhabitants of the planet earth ever get along? Wouldn't it be wonderful if world **peace** was a **fact** rather than merely a **vision** and a **hope**? You may have seen the bumper sticker that reads "Visualize Whirled Peas." Wouldn't it be sensational if we could simply spend our time imagining little green legumes spinning in perpetual motion rather than experience people dying daily because we haven't learned how to **cooperate**?

Horrible diseases such as smallpox, malaria, influenza, tuberculosis, AIDS, and a variety of plagues have wiped out huge segments of societies. We are in perpetual **fear** of human diseases' claiming our lives and the lives of others. Natural disasters including tsunamis, earthquakes, volcanoes, hurricanes, floods, fires, mudflows, avalanches, and more claim untold souls annually.

We are warned, "Don't talk to strangers;" "Lock your doors;" "Install your car alarm;" "Buy a burglar alarm;" "Never walk alone" (that's a great tune, isn't it); "Watch for pickpockets;" "Stay alert;" "Install security cameras;" blah, blah, blah, blah, blah, blah, blah, blah, blah! But has anyone ever told you where to look to find the most dangerous threat to your longevity? Has anyone ever told you where to look to find the most dangerous person you know? I will make it very clear. The mirror!

PEACE
Practicing
Effective
Attitudes
Calms
Everyone

FACT
Finding
Actual
Circumstances
True

VISION
Very
Intense
Statement
Indicating
Objectives
Necessary

HOPE
Harnessing
Optimism
Produces
Empowerment

COOPERATE
Change
Offers
Opportunities
People
Eventually
Realize
And
Teamwork
Excels

FEAR
Find
Each
Anxiety 'n
Repair

AMENDS
Always
Manage
Every
Negative
Discussion/
Sorry

This gets really simple. The mirror will help us clarify how we establish the feelings that measure our self-worth. The mirror will also help delineate the transgressions that affect our longevity.

If you agree with this concept, keep reading. If you don't agree, do yourself a huge favor. Lay down this book, go find a mirror, and stand right in front of it. Look yourself straight in the eye and ask yourself two questions. Am I totally happy with the person I see? What is getting in my way for complete personal happiness? Gulp!

Many years ago at a high-school graduation celebration, a student shared the following poem with the audience. This person had severely struggled with his self-image. As a result of his internal battles, he displayed an abrasive attitude towards others, and his relationships with his friends, the school family, and his immediate family were extremely strained. When he presented this heart-wrenching poem, he began making **amends** that changed his entire life. The people in attendance were reduced to tears

The Man in the Glass

When you've got what you want in your struggle
   for self
And the world makes you king for a day.
Just go to a mirror and look at yourself,
And see what that man has to say.

It isn't your parents or friends or your wife
Whose judgment upon you must pass;
The fellow whose verdict counts most in your life
Is the one staring back from the glass.

Some people may think you're a straight-shootin 'chum
And call you a wonderful guy;
But the man in the glass says you're only a bum
If you can't look him straight in the eye.

He's the fellow to please, never mind all the rest,
For he's with you clear to the end.
And you've past your most dangerous and difficult test
If the man in the glass is your friend.

You may fool the whole world down the pathway of years
And get pats on the back as you pass,
But your final reward will be heartache and tears
If you've **cheated** the man in the glass.

CHEATED
Circumventing
Honest
Efforts
Alleviates
Trust
Every
Day

Do you know which part of your body poses the biggest threat to a meaningful, fulfilling life and your final reward of longevity? I know you're thinking, "Well, it has to be my mind, or my mouth, or my tongue." Wrong! It is your elbow.

We humans bend elbows for lots and lots of reasons. We bend our elbows to drive, eat, drink sustaining fluids, consume alcohol, smoke cigarettes, do drugs, shoot guns—you name it. We bend our elbows to inflict damage to our bodies in many ways. The World Health Organization states that about one out of four people of the world is considered overweight. A third of all deaths globally are linked to weight, lack of exercise, and smoking.

Let's use eating as an example of how bending our elbow affects our balance of purpose, pleasure, and peace of mind. The purpose of eating is very obvious. We must consume food and fluid to sustain our lives. But wait—we also eat for other reasons. It gives us great pleasure. One of my wife's father's favorite sayings was "Eat till your belly hurts." That was another reason I loved Grandpa Joe!

What happens to our waistlines if we eat more than our bodies require for sustenance? Is it just like pouring more fuel into a vehicle than is needed? What if we regularly poured more fuel into a vehicle than the engine required for the amount of miles traveled? Imagine what the vehicle would look like if the fuel tank and the vehicle's body were expandable. If we pour more fuel into our bodies than we burn what happens to us? Duh! What happens to our self-image, our confidence, our feeling of self-worth? Is there a reason the majority of people in the developed world are attempting to diet to lose weight? Yes! Overeating is infringing on our peace of mind.

Food high in calories tastes fantastic; it has become more readily available at a more reasonable price. Advancements in food processing techniques have provided the world with inexpensive foods possessing a long shelf life and loaded with calories. The fast food industry provides convenient, inexpensive food that is extremely high in calories. The availability of this food provides us with opportunities for consuming copious amounts of calories at a very affordable price. Did we just describe a time bomb?

We eat for a purpose, to get nutrition. We eat because we receive pleasure; it comforts us. If we overeat, we infringe upon our peace of mind due to a lack of self-worth based on the less than desirable appearance that results. We find ourselves in a downward spiral: The more we eat, the more gravity affects our bodies, and the faster we fall into Fatsville. Our society is creating a pandemic of obese, unhealthy, and in the process, very unhappy people.

A recent dream of mine illuminated my personal battle of trying to inch back towards my marathon-running shape. I dreamed that on a recent night in late December while our neighborhood was aglow with colorful lights, our family, all snuggled in their beds, was startled by an incredible racket that erupted on our roof. (Gee, that was poetic!)

I ran outside and looked up to see what was happening. There was a man in a red suit with a long white beard in a sleigh being pulled by a bunch of animals adorned with bells. (I assumed they were wearing bells because their horns didn't work.)

I yelled up to him, "Why do you have those critters on my roof; who do you think you are?" He proudly proclaimed, "I'm Santa!" I replied "I don't care what you say your name is, ya old fat man! Get those reindeer off my roof!" He yelled back down, "Don't bother me, ya old fat elf!" He whistled, called his critters by name, and away they flew off towards the stars. Sure, I was upset that he woke me up in the middle of the night. Sure, I was pouting because there were no presents left under our tree. But I was really ticked because he called me a **fat elf**. But, ya know, I admit it: He was right. I was getting pretty porky, so after that late night encounter I made a difficult decision to attempt to "Forget All Treats, Eat Less Food."

Let's imagine that you are currently maintaining your ideal weight. For most of us, that's a fat chance (no pun intended). Let's do some simple caloric calculations to estimate what will happen if you add just 40 calories per day to your normal food intake for the next twenty years.

Forty calories. Hey, that's nothin', about four potato **chips.** Not four bags of chips, just four

FAT ELF
Forget
All
Treats
Eat
Less
Food

CHIPS
Calories
Help
Increase
People's
Size

chips, crackers, or snacking chips of just about any kind. Count them: one, two, three, four! Oh, you say you don't eat chips? Well, how about four French fries. Have you ever eaten just four chips or just four French fries?

If counting up to four makes it too tough, let's consider what just half a chocolate chip cookie added to your daily consumption will do to your svelte waistline; that's about 40 calories. Do you think there is a person on this planet who has ever had the self-control to eat just half a chocolate chip cookie? Is your mouth watering? Mine is!

Keep one fact in mind. It takes about 3,600 calories to add one pound of actual body weight, discounting water weight (remember, body mass). You may have surmised that you must burn about that same number of calories to lose one pound. You're right. It's really simple to lose a pound of body weight: Just run 36 miles! At a normal jogging rate, that will only take you about six hours—unless you stop to eat! We will continue talking about weight gain in round figures (no pun intended).

In one month, those four chips or fries or that half of a chocolate chip cookie would add only about five ounces to your weight—just a little over an ounce a week. No big deal. In the first year, you would gain only about four pounds. So what? Nobody will notice; your clothes will still fit. You'll still have space to stuff candy into your pockets! Do you see where we're headed with this? In ten years, you would gain 40 pounds, and in 20 years you would gain 80 pounds. You would then fit the definition of obese—all on just one extra mouthful of food per day!

Would you agree that the combination of our minds, bodies, and spirits can affect everything that we do, including overeating? Would you agree that our level of happiness can contribute to a healthy body weight? About fifteen years ago Steve Vaught accidentally killed two pedestrians while driving. Since then he has suffered from severe depression and his weight ballooned to 410 pounds. In an effort to lose weight and overcome depression, Steve walked 3,000 miles from Oceanside, California, to Manhattan, New York. He lost over one hundred pounds! After his trek he said, "I thought I had to lose the weight to be happy, but I've discovered you have to be happy to lose the weight." Mr. Vaught, thank you for being an incredible role model. Or shall we say in this case you have been an inspirational "roll" model?

Here are a couple of examples to help you understand some methods of controlling body weight. One summer while five of us were commercial fishing for salmon in Alaska, we ran out of supplies from the meat locker. We existed on the boat for three weeks without eating any meat other than fresh seafood. Yum! We consumed three, and sometimes four, balanced meals per day and an occasional dessert! We were different sizes and different ages, and we were exercising by working. However, all of us were shocked to discover that we had all lost ten pounds by the end of that three-week period!

Let's have a quick review. We ate three balanced meals a day at regular times, and our source of protein was fish. During the ensuing summers, we decided to cut way back on our meat orders, and we were able to continue enjoying our summer weight-loss programs.

FUN
Forget
Unnecessary
Nonsense

FEAR
Freezes
Every
Action....
Reconsider

For two other sensational summers, I was fortunate to have had the opportunity to be the conductor of a choir comprised of students from throughout the northwestern United States. We traveled and performed throughout Europe for nearly six weeks each summer. We had so much **fun**! Because our living expenses were prepaid, all of us ate the same food in the same restaurants throughout our tour. Talk about eating with no **fear**! We freely shared our food and drink during every meal. At each setting the women, kind souls that they were, would usually donate a healthy portion of their food to us guys. Get ready. All the guys lost between ten and fifteen pounds. On average, the women "found" just about what the guys lost. Life just ain't fair sometimes!

You can say "whatchawant" about diets and food fads until the cows come home. Most people agree that two elements should be considered in a weight-control strategy. Is it nutritious, and is it long lasting?

The world is full of the diet fads that claim "You can lose X number of pounds in X days." If they work for you, great; more power to you. I have come to some concrete conclusions regarding weight control based on personal experiences with "nonscientific control groups." (Now, there's an anomaly!)

Some Considerations in Weight Control:

- Emotional issues affect our desire to eat.
- Body size and metabolism rates influence minimum caloric requirements.
- Men are usually larger; consequently they usually burn more calories than women.

- Limit your intake of meat to primarily fish and fowl.
- Consume balanced meals with abundant whole grains, fruits, and vegetables.
- Maintain a regular meal schedule; eat only when seated.
- Avoid snacking on prepackaged treats.
- Severely limit your intake of high-calorie fast foods.
- Severely limit your intake of sugary drinks.
- Severely limit your intake of sweets.
- Exercise frequently.
- Consider chocolate medicinal.

While I was training for running marathons, I heeded my own advice regarding weight loss. By enacting the above formula, I was able to lose fifty pounds in six months and comfortably finish several marathons. I firmly **believe** that sensible eating habits coupled with an exercise program produce results.

BELIEVE
Bountiful
Experiences
Loved
If
Everyone
Visualizes
Eventualities

What are some other ways that our elbows cause problems for us? For as long as I can remember, both of my parents coughed and wheezed and spit up gross, ugly stuff; they were both heavy smokers. My three siblings also began smoking at early ages. Our small house maintained a perpetual cloud of secondhand smoke. The scientific studies had not yet begun to chronicle the debilitating health effects of smoking and secondhand smoke.

Fortunately, I viewed smoking as a filthy, smelly, nasty, disgusting, dangerous habit that severely afflicted both of my parents. Because of their bad example, I elected to avoid smoking cigarettes at all costs. My father practiced a horrible habit of smoking in bed. Lucky for us, we were able to put out the fires in his bed before they got out of control! This was long before smoke alarms hit the market.

HABITS
How
All
Beings
Imprint
Traits

Dad's smoking **habit** caused him breathing problems throughout his life and was a contributing factor in the declining health that led to his death. Mom's smoking habit killed her. I'll say that again. Mom's smoking habit killed her. Neither one of them could see the damage that was being inflicted on their bodies until it was too late. As the Roman poet Juvenal once said, "Refrain from doing ill; for one all powerful reason, lest our children should copy our misdeeds."

Emphysema ruled our mother's life for the two decades preceding her death. Because of her lifetime smoking habit, her heart became enlarged and worked overtime to compensate for the lung damage she had brought upon herself by smoking. Her lungs and circulatory system filled with fluid, and she basically drowned in that fluid, dying a horrible death. The medical term for this calamity is *congestive heart failure*.

If smoking is a concern for you or your acquaintances, there are several considerations in helping stop the habit. Store shelves are packed with proven products to help break the smoking habit.

Here is another plan of action that I recommend you strongly consider. If you currently smoke and need help deciding if you desire to quit, visit a hospital and ask if you can tour the pulmonary ward. Don't worry, it will be easy to locate; it will be a very large area. Spend some time visiting with the patients. You will undoubtedly determine that many of them will never walk out of that facility. Imagine that your current habit will help you to become a patient in that ward someday. Are you looking forward to that day? Perhaps this experience will encourage you to seek help and, hopefully, enable you to stop smoking.

How do I feel about my parents' addiction to smoking? You know that losing friends and loved ones is, beyond a doubt, the most difficult part of living. The pain of loss lasts forever. Do you remember what my father said during his last few days? "Death is the one price that we have to pay for living." He was absolutely correct. However, we do have some control over when that price must be paid. Wouldn't you like to pay that price as far in the future as possible, so that many more people will have a chance to benefit from knowing you? "Mom and Dad, while you were killing yourselves with cigarettes, you may not have realized the monumental disappointment that was developing within my heart. Because of your premature deaths, my children never had the opportunity to know you and to love you, their grandparents."

With great pride, I'd like to report that my three siblings have been empowered to break their addiction to nicotine. The route I traveled to avoid the fatal effects of smoking was much easier; I didn't begin!

As with many teachers, my door has always been open to assist students with their trials and tribulations. It took me several decades to conclude that one of the paramount goals of education is simply to help others connect their emotions with their intelligence.

Years ago, a very respectful, appreciative sophomore discussed several of her home problems with me. We spent a considerable amount of time trying to discover solutions to her situation. There seemed to be more roadblocks to understanding Sarah's dilemma than I could negotiate. I finally advised her to seek additional help from one of our school counselors, which she did.

Months later, upon the death of her father, Sarah's personal issues came to the fore in a very dramatic way. The night before his funeral, Sarah called our house around midnight. I've always encouraged students to contact me if they are in a crisis. Through her anguished outbursts, I determined that she desperately needed to meet and talk. We arranged to have her older sister accompany her to a 24-hour restaurant so the three of us could meet.

It took some time; however, Sarah was finally able to identify the source of her emotional trauma. At last, she blurted out, "My dad's being buried tomorrow, and I don't know if I should love him or hate him because he physically abused me since I was a very little girl!"

The mystery of her emotional upheaval finally surfaced. Needless to say, in all the psychology courses, sessions, and study I have absorbed, I was not prepared to answer the question she had posed. Into the wee hours of the morning, we discussed methods of separating her father's actions from the person she had loved before the problems began. That was certainly a monumental undertaking in this case of severe **abuse**. I pointed out that she had only one chance to attend her father's fu-

ABUSE
All
Beings
Underestimate
Some
Eventualities

neral. After much soul searching, she decided to attend. Sarah also agreed to continue her sessions with her mental health professional.

Throughout high school, Sarah attempted to display signs of normalcy, but I understood that she was experiencing a great deal of deep emotional turmoil. Everyone in our school family paid close attention to her condition. During this entire process, I kept her counselor, family, and our school staff apprised of my perceptions of her delicate emotional balance.

One day I received a frantic phone call from the high-school principal. He said, "Bruce, get to the main office as fast as you can. Sarah is tearing the place apart, and we have the police on the way!" I bolted out of the choir room and raced to the office; Sarah was going ballistic. The staff was attempting to physically subdue her—to no avail. I sat down in a chair and calmly said, "Sarah, come over here and sit by me." She immediately and very calmly heeded my order; if only all students could be so responsive.

Two police officers arrived and began to arrest her on a multitude of civil charges. I interrupted their procedure. (You should file these actions under the category of "please don't try this yourself!") After a considerable amount of deliberation, I convinced the school administration and the arresting officers that Sarah should be entrusted to my care. Whew!

The school nurse and I transported this very ill young lady to a mental hospital in a nearby city. The legal ramifications of this action were astronomical. But I just kept remembering what my mom always told me. "Bruce if your **heart** tells you it's **right**, don't be concerned what others say." Mom, I hope we proved that you were correct!

HEART
Help
Everyone
Achieve
Respect
Today

RIGHT
Respecting
Integrity
Grants
Honor
Today

DOPE
Does
Overuse
Paralyze
Empowerment

DOPER
Does
Overuse
Produce
Extinguishing
Results

HIGH
Help
Individuals
Get
Happy

DRUGS
Do
Results
Ultimately
Guarantee
Success

BUSY
Bosses
Usually
Stress
You

WORK
We
Only
Respect
Kindness

The staff at the mental hospital diagnosed Sarah with paranoid schizophrenia. She spent years stuck in the revolving door of mental institutions. I visited her as often as possible, and 'til this day she still calls us on a nearly annual basis. Sarah's mystery finally began to unravel when she became mentally balanced enough to discuss the tantrum she had thrown in the high school office.

Sarah explained that she had been smoking illegal drugs with her boyfriend the night previous to the office incident. We concluded that her fragile emotional condition, in combination with the **dope** she was smoking, was much more powerful than her **doper** boyfriend could have imagined. That single encounter fried this beautiful young lady's mind. She has spent decades trying to recover from that evening of getting **high** on a combination of **drugs** that were unknown to her.

Some of my fondest memories directing choirs are of a series of groups during the seventies and early eighties at Clover Park High School about an hour's drive south of Seattle. During those years, the school population was about 1,800 students in grades ten through twelve.

Because of the large student population, many students were available to participate in the choral program. Our curriculum consisted of a full day of choir classes; ensembles and soloists rehearsed before and after school. Life was simpler then; not as many students had jobs other than school, so they were readily available to perform throughout the area on nonschool time. This was a magical time in their lives and in mine.

The groups were invited to perform at many

venues. Because we had so many invitations, we were able to be quite selective about when and where we offered our music. We avoided weekend performances, and we did not perform during vacation periods. We perpetually attempted to balance our purpose, pleasure, and peace of mind. Even though we turned down about seventy-five percent of our performance invitations, we still were extremely **busy**. One December we had twenty-five major performances on our list. It was certainly a lot of hard **work,** but we had so much **fun**!

The choirs were also selected to perform at several music educator conferences. One of the performances that will be vividly etched in our minds forever was a Washington All State Music Conference held in February 1978 at A. C. Davis High School in Yakima, Washington.

That year, the Clover Park Concert Choir consisted of 66 students. Almost all of them had taken private voice lessons and had sung solos at the league solo contest or other venues. The students had a tremendous amount of performance experience. For developing a sense of self-worth, there is absolutely no substitute for learning how to **work**.

During the winter vacation, I was at home enjoying our choirs' holiday television special when I was struck by the realization of the magnificent quality of the production. It wasn't just the songs they were singing; it wasn't just the way they were performing; and it certainly wasn't just my conducting. It was a force much greater than any single facet of the process: It was the **music**.

The music was the creative discipline. Learning how to create music had taught the students the

FUN
Forget
Unnecessary
Nonsense

WORK
We
Only
Respect
Kindness

MUSIC
Mankind's
Ultimate
Study
In
Creation

JOYS
Just
Offer
Your
Spirit

TEAMWORK
Tolerance
Empowers
All
Members;
We
Only
Respect
Kindness

CHOIR
Caring
Hearts
Offer
Inspired
Relationships

IMPROVE
Individuals
Make
Progress
Rewarding
Our
Valiant
Efforts

COST
Concentrating
Only
Saves
Time

CONFIDENCE
Changing
Our
Negative
Fears
Invites
Delightful
Experiences
Never
Considered
Easy

work ethic to develop their individual performance skills. The music had taught them to be tolerant of the other members in the choir. Their work ethic had enabled them to lift their level of achievement to magnified heights. They had learned to share their **joys** in music with the audience; the singers were such a warm, loving group of people. It was an absolute honor for all of us to be part of that musical family, and we cherished every moment that we were together. I was deeply moved watching this magnificent choir display the true meaning of **teamwork** to hundreds of thousands of viewers via the magic of television.

In January, the concert **choir** students decided that they wanted to "ramp up" their efforts to prepare for the upcoming Washington Music Educators' Conference performance. So we added after-school rehearsals to our already busy schedule. We invited some of the best and brightest choral conductors in the area to join us in rehearsals to help us **improve**.

The kids were learning to concentrate at any **cost**. They diligently refined the fundamentals of their music. We also worked on our level of **confidence**. One day, I asked the group, "How should we view performing for hundreds of music educators? We'll need to be at our very best, and that won't happen if **nerves** and **fear** get in our way." Jeff Howe had an **idea** and raised his hand. In his slight Southern drawl he explained, "This will be really easy; the folks we'll be singing for will be very appreciative. They know better than anyone else how difficult it is to get a group of teenagers to work together and present a **perfect** performance. Let's help the music educators remember why they selected making music with kids as their career!"

The bus trip to Yakima was a monumental occasion. The students had worked so hard, and they were so excited to share their **talents**. To this day, I even remember what I was wearing on the bus; it was a new outfit to fit my reduced body size. To **honor** the students' hard work, I told them that I would lose a bunch of weight so they wouldn't have a **fat** director standing in front of them for their big performance. I had severely reduced my caloric intake for several months, without additional exercise. I was skinny as a noodle, proving that **desire** does matter.

The performance at A. C. Davis High School was held in a beautiful auditorium with natural wood features and great acoustics. The reverb in the room was absolutely perfect to enhance choral tone; we knew all of the elements required for a perfect performance were coming together. Maurice Skones, conductor of the Choir of the West from Pacific Lutheran University believed two elements are required for a sensational choral performance: **attitude** and acoustics. We knew we possessed both.

The choir entered this beautiful auditorium by walking from the back and processing in two rows up the aisles to the risers on the stage. We had spent hours practicing this very important portion of the performance; we had only one chance to make our first impression. Our flamboyant entrance was choreographed perfectly. The kids began sharing their love of themselves and one another through their music; the audience became riveted on their magnificent musical performance.

NERVES
Negative
Energy
Ruins
Visions;
Envision
Success

FEAR
Freezes
Every
Action....
Reconsider

IDEA
Inspiration
Deserves
Everyone's
Attention

PERFECT
Pursuing
Everything
Right,
Forgetting
Every
Care
Tactfully

TALENT
To
Achieve,
Latent
Energy
Needs
Training

HONOR
Helping
Others
Needing
Our
Respect

FAT
Forget
All
Treats

DESIRE
Does
Everyone
Strive
In
Reaching
Excellence

ATTITUDE
All
Terrific
Thoughts
Incorporate
True
Unrelenting
Dedication to
Excellence

PAIN
People
Always
Inherit
Nerves

At the conclusion of the half-hour concert, we exited the stage, retracing our steps through the audience. The students were treated to the recognition of a lifetime; the audience of nearly a thousand music educators was standing and applauding with tears cascading down their faces. We had attained our goal of reaching their hearts to remind them why they had selected music education as their career!

As we went outside, the kids hoisted me into the air and were spinning me around as though we had just won the Super Bowl. The audience filed out and congratulated the students on their stirring performance. Many of my role models and mentors were in the mass of people who were congregating to honor the students: Raleigh McVicker, one of the most magnificent teachers imaginable and the person who convinced me to start singing at Olympic College in Bremerton, Washington. Maurice Skones, one of the world's premier choral conductors from the Choir of the West at Pacific Lutheran University. Bill Bissel, the world-renowned marching-band director from the University of Washington in Seattle. The joy they experienced watching the students' success was bubbling over beyond belief. We had overcome all the **pain** of the **hard work**; a **true** sense of **dignity** enveloped us!

A few days after that performance of a lifetime, when my feet were closer to touching the earth again, I had a very memorable discussion with our assistant superintendent. Mr. Smith was very kind in congratulating me on the choir's success. He pointed out what good public relations it was for the school district and how it helped the image of the school for passing bonds and levy tax measures.

I thanked him for his kind words and said, "Dick, I thoroughly agree with you; there are many benefits from this choir's fine reputation. But do you know something? Do you know what the greatest benefit to those individual kids has been? What they learned about how to work to gain a feeling of self-worth will stay with them throughout their lives. They have learned to overcome their fears and to make the most of themselves. They have learned that building successful relationships and developing a strong work ethic lead to a high level of self-worth, which results in opening the doors to a lifetime of true happiness."

Dick recanted his original statement regarding the district's image and public relations. Then he said, "Bruce, I am in absolute agreement with you . . . thanks . . . now I thoroughly understand where you're coming from; we're in this for kids and what we can do to enhance their feelings of self-worth!"

No money was disbursed at the music conference performance; no prizes were awarded; and no trophies were collected. Our **reward** was the feeling of **pride** that we received by reaching our **goal** of a perfect musical performance.

Let's take a giant leap and view what can occur at the opposite end of the spectrum from the euphoria we felt after that choral performance of a lifetime. Several years later, I left a district administrative post I had held for many years to become the choir director at Stadium High School. Yes, I decided to return to my favorite activity in life—making music with kids! Stadium is a majestic French Chateau-style castle perched on a hill overlooking Puget Sound in Tacoma, Washington.

HARDWORK
Happiness
Awaits
Relentless
Desire;
We
Only
Respect
Kindness

TRUE
To
Rely
Upon
Everything

DIGNITY
Depicting
Integrity
Granting
Nobility
In
Thy
Years

REWARD
Realizing
Everyone's
Work
Assures
Recognition
Deserved

PRIDE
People
Respect
Individuals
Delivering
Excellence

GOALS
Greatness
Only
Awaits
Labor—
Staaaaaart

TRAGEDY
Terrible
Results
Accentuate
Grief
Everyone
Deliriously
Yearns

GUN
Give
Up
Now

One evening while our family was gathered around the dinner table, I received a horrific telephone call from the school. An official informed me that a **tragedy** had occurred late that afternoon at the school. After school was dismissed, a student whom I did not know had committed suicide in a restroom near the choir room. It was later discovered the despondent student had told several of his friends that day that he had a **gun** in his possession. The students failed to alert any school personnel for fear the desperate fellow would have been expelled from school. He had been reduced to committing the ultimate display of lacking a feeling of self-worth; he had elected to exit this earth.

Because many of the choir students were his friends, they voted to share their music at his final service. There is a strong possibility the service may never have been necessary if we could have had more of an opportunity to share our love with him before that fateful day.

There are simply no words to describe the feelings of helplessness, guilt, loss, and despair that plagued our entire school community with the death of this student. He had successfully robbed himself, his family, and his friends of his love on this earth. This young man had so sadly taken the ultimate step in signifying his lack of self-worth. In his cry for help, he acknowledged that the person we hopefully learn to love the most is also the person we know the best on this earth. The person we hopefully love the most is also the most dangerous person we know on this earth . . . our self.

CHAPTER 12

TEAMWORK
<u>T</u>olerance <u>E</u>mpowers <u>A</u>ll <u>M</u>embers; <u>W</u>isdom <u>O</u>ffers <u>R</u>enewed <u>K</u>indness

John Wooden has been one of the greatest coaches of all time. During his tenure, basketball teams from the University of California, Los Angeles (UCLA), amassed ten National Collegiate Athletic Association championships—a feat in sports many feel will never be equaled.

Why was coach Wooden so incredibly successful? There were certainly many reasons. For openers, he believed in what he termed the **CST** principle, the three essential ingredients in any group activity: conditioning, skills, and teamwork. He unequivocally believed that teamwork was by far the most important aspect of the equation.

CST
Conditioning
Skills
Teamwork

Here is the list of "normal expectations" coach Wooden employed to develop his concept of teamwork with his UCLA basketball players:

- Be a gentleman at all times.
- Never criticize, nag, or razz a teammate.
- Be a team player always.
- Never be selfish, jealous, envious, or egotistical.
- Earn the right to be proud and confident.
- Never expect favors, alibi, or make excuses.
- Never lose faith or patience.
- Courtesy and politeness are a small price to pay for the good will and affection of others.

- Acquire peace of mind by becoming the best that you are capable of becoming.

Wow! Was coach Wooden listing these expectations of his players for just their basketball experiences or for their entire lives? Does this list of expectations provide us with a template of how to live our lives and to help us get along with others? Does it describe many of life's goals? Does it include possibly the greatest of life's goals, which is peace of mind?

Baseball Hall of Fame catcher Yogi Berra once said, "You can observe a lot by watching." Perhaps he was watching one of coach Wooden's teams when he coined that phrase. To gain a clearer picture of how teams function effectively, let's take Yogi's advice and look more closely at group dynamics to help us understand the mechanics of team interactions.

A team is certainly much more than just a group of people running around chasing a ball while wearing numbers on their backs. A team is formed any time two or more people are interacting together. Our entire existence as human beings is structured around team concepts.

We have three choices to guide our actions in every team situation. We are always deciding if we are going to fight, flee, or flow. If we decide to **fight**, the fight usually begins with an argument. Three wise men have made some excellent points about arguments. American writer and speaker Dale Carnegie said that the only way to win an argument is not to **argue**. Rabbi Richard Rosenthal from Tacoma, Washington, said the best way to create an

FIGHT
Ferocious
Insults
Generate
High
Tensions

ARGUE
Always
Repeating
Garbage
Unnerves
Everyone

argument is to try to have the last word. And Louis Brandeis, a former U.S. Supreme Court justice, said that behind every argument is someone's ignorance.

An ancient Chinese Proverb states, "He who strikes the first blow admits he lost the argument."

How do we avoid arguments in our day-to-day activities? Let's look at a simple example. An acquaintance of mine named Frank has had limited fishing experience. Recently, Frank was extremely excited about one of his latest angling adventures. He was just bubbling over with enthusiasm as he related his story about catching salmon during the fall of the year in Puget Sound near Seattle. He told me that the salmon he was angling for were jumping and swirling in a large school near the mouth of a stream; they were preparing to travel upstream to spawn. I asked him what kind of salmon he caught, and he said, "They were blackmouth." I kindly pointed out that blackmouth are immature king salmon that are at least one year from their spawning time. In the fall of the year, blackmouth would be out toward the middle of the bay, feeding in deeper water.

Frank's exuberance continued to overflow as he related the story about catching his limit of salmon. At the conclusion of his story, I asked, "Now, you're sure those weren't silvers?" He replied, "I've been fishing all my life; I know the difference between cohos and silvers!"

Cohos and silvers are different names for the same species of salmon. They are a different species from blackmouth. Are you as confused as Frank? This gets really confusing; hang on.

Six species of salmon inhabit the waters of Washington State: kings, silvers, chums, pinks, reds, and Atlantics. It's tough enough to tell the six species from one another. It is especially challenging when you start calling them by their other names. For example, king salmon are also called blackmouth, tyees, chinooks, tules, upriver brights, pigs, hogs, hens, bucks, hawgs, slabs, whites, reds, marbles, smileys, keepers, larges, mediums, smalls, tankers, legals, sublegals, netters, springs, springers, hatcheries, natives, falls, cruisers, feeders, chromers, boots, slimers, smokers, and spawners. The list goes on and on. That's just one species; the other species also have a variety of vernacular titles!

It was very obvious that Frank was confused about the species of salmon he was catching. They could not have been blackmouth; I knew they were silvers. Did I argue with him? Absolutely not!

What purpose would I have fulfilled by arguing with him? Would the outcome of winning the argument improve my purpose, pleasure, and peace of mind? No! Did my ego need to be fed to prove that I have spent my life catching tons of salmon in Washington, Canada, and Alaska? No! Was our discussion structured like a sports contest to select a winner? No! Was I going to employ the sports contest mentality to defeat him at all costs? No! Would I have staved off a nuclear war? No! Would an argument have eroded the joy that Frank received from his fishing expedition? Yes! Would an argument have eroded our friendship? Duh!

EGOS
Everybody
Gags
On
Selfishness

Do we become embroiled in arguments in an attempt to bolster our pride and inflate our **egos** to hopefully overcome our feelings of inferiority? Was I capable of practicing a level of humility with Frank? What happens to the basic concepts of teamwork if team members are perpetually attempting to inflate their own egos—especially if those attempts are focused towards proving that others are wrong or inferior?

You know what happens? If we are involved with people who operate in this manner, we employ a simple defense mechanism. We avoid those people in the future, and we elect to reject their future involvements with us. And away goes the hope of having a cohesive team.

Are there times to take a stand when a disagreement needs to be settled? Certainly! That's why we have court systems. Here are several steps to consider before "going to the mat" with someone:

1. Study and select your battle; know what resolution you would like to attain; remember getting **mad** won't help.
2. Avoid attacking individual personalities; focus on the facts involved in the issue.
3. Discuss the options for resolving the issue as soon as possible at the lowest level.
4. Proceed through the appropriate chain of command.
5. Know when to end your pursuit or when it's appropriate to seek assistance.
6. Throughout the entire process, ask yourself, "Is this worth the emotional energy and resources that I must expend in hopes of reaching the desired outcome?"

What does fighting and conflict do for the effectiveness of a team? Are we much more productive if we expend our energies trying to **help** one

MAD
Meaness
Always
Destroys

HELP
Hurry
Everyone
Loves
Progress

PROGRESS
People
Reform
Or
Garner
Refinement
Establishing
Some
Success

LAZY
Losers
Always
Zap
Ya

WORK
We
Only
Respect
Kindness

FEEL
Fear
Eventually
Eliminates
Love

JOYS
Just
Open
Your
Soul

another rather than trying to hinder **progress**? Is arguing simply a form of negativism? Remember, most people are allergic to negativism; avoid it if possible! Have you considered that arguing and displaying negativity many times is simply a symptom of being **lazy**? One day in a seventh-grade choir rehearsal, Ashley summed up this concept very succinctly. She said, "Don't be a jerk, go to **work**!"

One consideration involving teamwork revolves around deciding when and if we should leave the groups to which we belong. Why do we switch schools, jobs, community organizations, marriages, families, etc.? Because we usually **feel** that the negativity is not commensurate with the **joys** received.

Certainly there are many reasons people flee from group settings; however, it usually comes down to not being appreciated, valued, and respected as an individual. Study any organization that has a very small turnover of members, and measure that organization's level of displaying respect, showing appreciation, and demonstrating that its members are valued.

While I attended high school, Mrs. Hilliard, my contemporary world problems teacher, explained it this way. If we have a problem with any kind of a group we have three choices:

• Change ourselves.
• Change our situation.
• Change a little of both.

One day, while I was teaching a middle-school boys choir class, we discussed how group dynamics actually work in classes, sports, choirs, families, scouts, the workplace, and elsewhere. We discussed the steps needed for successful teamwork to evolve. It was a day of great enlightenment for all . . . especially for me.

The boys settled on five steps that they labeled the "flow formula." They decided that in every team setting someone needs to:

1. *Fire up the flow.* The leader, captain, parent, boss, coach, etc., establishes the goals, ground rules, and expectations for the project. In a group that functions properly, members will have an opportunity to
2. *Feed the flow* by making suggestions, adding comments, brainstorming, or supporting the leader of the endeavor. Hopefully, other group members will be observing the process and
3. *Follow the flow* by embellishing and acting on the suggestions and observations. When, and if (and it is usually when) someone
4. *Freezes the flow*, then someone will need to jump in and
5. *Fix the flow.*

I learned a lot about teamwork when I played football in high school. Our team had an absolutely perfect record. We were 10 and 0. **Oops**, maybe I should explain; we lost ten and won none. Did I learn a lot about teamwork? I learned that when someone freezes the flow, it needs to be fixed. Throughout life, we learn what to do and what not to do. My high school football experience taught me a great lesson of many things not to do when developing a team!

OOPS
Opportunities
Often
Pass
Swiftly

IDEA
Inspiration
Deserves
Everyone's
Attention

TRY
To
Respect
Yourself

IDIOT
Individual's
Debilitating
Ideas
Offends
Team

Let's study an example of a team process that works, even though it may take some time to come to fruition. Our two sons attended a private school that is affiliated with our church. One night during a school-wide parents' meeting, we were asked to form small groups and to develop an **idea**. We were asked to **try** to determine feasible methods of thanking the parishioners for the financial support they provided to the school.

About twenty parents were sitting in our circle on the floor. Our circle chairperson spelled out the challenge facing us to thank the parishioners. That person had fired up the flow. Many suggestions were made to feed the flow. People suggested sending thank-you cards to homes, making announcements in church, making signs, etc. Jumping on board to follow the flow, I said, "I know this isn't the answer, but wouldn't it be great if we walked out into the parking lot after the church service and our cars had been washed? Maybe we could bring in fire trucks to help us?" Guess what happened. Those people jumped on me like I was a complete **idiot**. They were prime examples of how easy it is to freeze the flow. Much to my disappointment, nobody in the group attempted to fix the flow that evening. Needless to say, I quickly lost my enthusiasm for attempting to add to the team brainstorming session.

Will it help to remember the steps if we list them this way?

- Fire up the flow
- Feed the flow
- Follow the flow
- Freeze the flow
- Fix the flow

About two months later as we approached our car after a Sunday morning service, we noticed a small handcrafted card placed under our windshield blade. We opened the envelope and it read, "Dear parishioners. Thank you so much for supporting our school. I sure love going to school here! Katie, 2nd grade." It took her several weeks, but Katie had accomplished number five in the teamwork flowchart. Sweet little Katie had been a part of fixing the flow.

Bart Starr, one of the greatest team players in the history of professional sports, has received many accolades for his personal triumphs on the football field. The Hall of Fame quarterback for the Green Bay Packers was selected as the Most Valuable Player when the Packers won the first two Super Bowls. When asked about the value of teamwork to their coach, Vince Lombardi, Bart said, "Lombardi explained that some of the players on the team are going to be famous, some obscure, but everyone was equally important. For us to succeed, we had to place our personal goals behind those of the team. We had to pick each other up and push each other to higher levels."

Mr. Lombardi, I'll bet that you would heartily approve of the way little Katie fixed the flow!

CHAPTER 13

INTEGRITY
Individuals Never Trust Evil;
Golden Rule Inspires Their Years

At Santa Clara University in California, a researcher recently conducted a study of 1,500 business managers that revealed what workers value most in a supervisor. Employees said they respected a leader who shows competence, has the ability to inspire workers, and is skillful in providing direction.

But there was a fourth quality they admired even more—integrity. Above all else, workers wanted a manager whose word was good—one who was known for honesty and one whom they could trust.

> If your word is "good as gold"
> And your actions prove it true,
> Others hearing what you say
> Know they can depend on you.
> —Hess

Serving as supervisor of music for Clover Park School District, providing music opportunities for 13,000 students was a management position dream come true. I remember shaking hands with Mr. Jack Fields and Mr. Jack Kunz, my mentors while I was student teaching at Lake Washington High School as they said, "We'll be coming to you looking for a job when you're supervisor." Their confidence in my management and leadership potential helped build my **confidence** at an impressionable young age.

CONFIDENCE
Changing
Our
Negative
Fears
Invites
Delightful
Experiences
Never
Considered
Easy

BOSS
Big
On
Securing
Success

DEMAND
Do
Everything
Management
Asks
No
Discussion

BUSY
Bosses
Usually
Stress
You

FAIRLY
Fervent
Attitudes
Including
Respect
Lead
You

A management position provides the opportunity for a person to be a leader. However, I learned that leadership is much more than simply managing human and financial resources. True leadership is inspiring others to go beyond their self-imposed limitations. John Maxwell, writer and motivational speaker, says, "The difference between being a leader and a manager is inspiration." As I reflect back upon those times, I am beginning to understand that a leader's integrity is measured by the level of success achieved while inspiring others to be successful.

When I assumed the district position, a high percentage of students were involved in the band and choral programs. Things were really cookin' in those departments. The orchestral program was all right; however, the string teachers bless their hearts, were trying to determine methods to bolster the number of students playing stringed instruments.

This was about the time my **boss** placed a **demand** on me to schedule the elementary instrumental music classes outside the regular school day. Have you noticed a major conflict? The folks up top were telling me to reduce the music instruction program as the staff was trying to expand the offerings. Does the term *downsizing* sound familiar? So I got really **busy** to do what I could to rescue the floundering ship.

We held a series of meetings over several months and developed a procedure for making decisions. Remember, results will be accepted only if plans and procedures have been executed **fairly**. We surveyed other school districts, and we held a series of meetings with parents, teachers, principals, and district administrators. We met with anyone who was interested in helping us revise the music program.

We developed several detailed options and presented them to the superintendent, Mr. Alexander. He decided to accept the option to expand the music staff to accommodate projected student enrollments. Yeah!

While I was struggling with a way to increase student participation in the string program, I was struck with an **idea**. I felt that it was not enough for students just to watch other students play or to talk about playing. The future orchestral musicians needed some world-class role models! It took eighteen months of planning and hard work to make the role model **dream** come true. One of the keys to realizing the dream was to procure financial backing in order to guarantee my **plan**. I knocked on lots of doors, and I got used to hearing **no**. I got used to people giving me plenty of reasons why they would not donate funds to enable kids to attend an assembly.

Finally, Mr. Highsmith, an executive from a local bank, said, "Bruce, I know you really have the kids' best interests at heart. Don't worry about the finances. Our bank will take care of any shortfalls that you might encounter." I wanted to cry. . . . I knew we could make it happen!

Next, I began negotiating a plan for thousands of students to witness a performance by the ninety-five member Seattle Symphony! The staff at Pacific Lutheran University kindly agreed to donate the use of Olson Auditorium for the events. Consequently, 3,200 students from seven local school districts were able to marvel at an hour-long concert of one of the finest musical organizations in the world.

IDEA
Inspiration
Deserves
Everyone's
Attention

DREAMS
Desire
Reflects
Eventual
Achievements
Magically
Secured

PLAN
Please
Learn
All
Necessities

NO
Nice
Opportunity

We staged this magnificent annual event for five years. Guess what happened to the numbers of students enrolled in the orchestral programs in the seven participating school districts? They went through the roof. We tripled the numbers at Clover Park. Is this a perfect example of how important role models are in our lives?

A few days before one of the concerts, a large contingent of our armed forces was deployed on a peace-keeping mission to the Middle East. During this time, our family traveled to Seattle to attend a monster truck show in the Kingdome. Just before the trucks started roaring, the announcer said, "Will everyone please rise for 'The Star Spangled Banner.'"

I knew that with the huge surge of patriotism being displayed throughout the country the audience would blast the roof off with their singing (ironically, the roof, along with the entire building was intentionally blasted a few years later). The announcer continued, "Please listen to . . . " I was so upset that I turned him off right there. Instead of singing, forty thousand Americans stood there and listened to a recording of someone else warbling through our National Anthem. I was really—as Ivar Haglund, founder of Ivar's Acres of Clams restaurant, would say—steamed! But it gave me an idea.

The next day, I called the folks at the Seattle Symphony and explained my desire to have the symphony begin our program with "The Star Spangled Banner." They had their doubts that the song could be performed, considering the short notice.

The executives from the symphony met and then informed me that there were too many obstacles to overcome for the anthem to be performed. They said they couldn't do it. Whoops, I heard an apostrophe *T*. So I told them, "I'll make you a deal. The piece will be performed, but it will be sung by 3,200 kids, many of them with parents deployed overseas, and I'll be leading the singing."

The day of the concert at Pacific Lutheran University, a very dear friend of mine, Jim Snyder, made an announcement at the beginning of the event. Mr. Snyder said, "Will everyone please rise and join in singing 'The Star Spangled Banner.'" After the announcement, while standing at the rear of the orchestra I quietly blew the starting note on a pitch pipe. I proceeded through the center of the orchestra with the pitch in mind to begin leading the kids in the song.

Suddenly, just before I reached the microphone, I realized the string players were sounding a different pitch for me. I used their pitch to begin leading the audience in singing. As the tune progressed, the full Seattle Symphony Orchestra gradually joined in playing the National Anthem. I instinctively raised my arms and began conducting as the hair on the back of my neck started standing up, goose bumps began blanketing my body, and chills ran rampant up and down my spine. I experienced what, to this day, was the conducting highlight of my musical career.

John C. Maxwell, American author and motivational speaker, would more than likely have categorized the symphony situation under his "management myth." He believes that the difference between being a manager and being a leader are two different things. He contends that most understandings about leadership are really about management. The act of managing is maintaining systems and processes. Leadership is influencing people to follow. Did conducting the National Anthem exemplify much more than managing a concert and waving arms in the air? Was this an example of true leadership, inspiring others to follow by example?

The former Chrysler Chairman and CEO Lee Iacocca would probably have also defined this event as an act of leadership. He explained leadership by influence this way: "Sometimes even the best manager is like the little boy with the big dog, waiting to see where the dog wants to go so that he can take him there."

While I was the choir director at Stadium High School in Tacoma, a student teacher named Glen Johnson very kindly questioned my rehearsal techniques. He could not figure out why I simply asked the advanced choir students to walk around the cafeteria in circles while singing. He felt that I should have been much more of a micromanager.

He thought that my job as a conductor was to thoroughly instruct the choir students and show them, with gestures, what I wanted them to do. He was extremely puzzled by my leadership style. Glen's questioning led to a series of long discussions exploring how inspiring others can **empower** them to reach their potential.

The cafeteria was the most magnificent rehearsal room imaginable. A portion of the room was circular, creating great acoustics. The room's massive windows overlooked Puget Sound, with Mt. Rainier in the distance. That rehearsal room had one of the greatest views in the world!

EMPOWER
Everyone
Makes
Pertinent
Observations
With
Every
Response

Throughout the rehearsals the students walked in circles and conducted themselves while they were singing. They thoroughly understood the fundamentals of developing a sensational choir because they were all very experienced musicians. I certainly did not need to micromanage their efforts. They concentrated on their posture, vocal technique, pitch, tone, phrasing, word stress, syllabic stress, etc., as they relished the beautiful sights spanning before them. During the rehearsals, we discussed all the **joys** they had received in their lives and how they could share those **joys** with others through their music. They learned to thoroughly **enjoy** the mystery and the magic of making music. Consequently, the musical message was personal. It was about their experiences, and it was about attempting to answer the questions in their lives. They were truly empowered by their **music**.

Replays of the Stadium High School award winning holiday television specials are aired every year throughout the holidays. As I watch those shows, I continue to marvel at the connection between the conductor and the choir, and I realize one major component of their success. Their conductor was just like that little boy with the big dog. He figured out where the choir wanted to go, and he helped them get there.

JOYS
Just
Open
Your
Soul

JOYS
Just
Offer
Your
Spirit

ENJOY
Everyone
Now
Journey
Over
Yonder

MUSIC
Mankind's
Ultimate
Study
In
Creation

CHAPTER 14

COMMUNICATION
Creating Only Manageable Methods,
Understanding Negative Innuendos Carefully,
And Teaming Individuals On Needs

Even though communication technology is continually changing, the basic principles of human interactions will never alter. We are perpetually attempting to refine and balance our methods of communicating with one another. Do you remember the simple fact that we were born with one mouth and two ears? The basic formula of receiving twice the information we emit is sage advice to follow. How does this formula for practicing effective listening skills apply in real life?

Steve Ballmer, the CEO of Microsoft, has said that the number-one ingredient for success in life and business is to practice agility—the methods we use to move people from one location to another to allow for more effective communication. He refers to highway systems, rail systems, air transportation systems, and other transportation systems. You're saying, "Wait just a minute here; why is a leader in communications technology so concerned with transportation?" Mr. Ballmer simply believes that you still need to be able to look people straight in the eye to best understand what they mean. Yes, Steve believes that the best way to practice successfully understanding others is to be able to communicate in person—face-to-face.

We use the term networking for linking computers via wires and through the airways. We use the same term for linking people to other people. To understand the impact of networking on a human scale, think about the jobs you have held or will hold throughout your life, the community organizations you've belonged to, and the hobbies you have enjoyed.

Do you remember the person who influenced you to become involved with that job, activity, or hobby? Sure you do! That's an example of communication and leadership. You followed other people because you respected their integrity and you realized the personal benefits you could receive by being involved. It's simply human nature. When you spoke with the person who influenced you, it was probably a face-to-face meeting. Reading other people's physical reactions is key to understanding their perspective. Consider terming those face-to-face meetings "wet working." Your meeting probably included a beverage or, better yet, a beverage and food! You might consider that networking is using your computer, and wet working is talking directly with people!

SMILE
Sure
Makes
It
Lots
Easier

NICE
Never
Insult
Compliment
Everyone

When you were a child and visited someone, started school, or joined an organization, your parents probably gave you some very simple advice. If you are a parent, an employer, a coach, etc, I'll bet you have given your followers the same advice: "**smile** and be **nice.**" Those two concepts have surfaced on a regular basis in the hundreds of hours I have spent interviewing people regarding their success.

A few years ago while rehearsing an adult choir, I was attempting to convince the vocalists to smile while they were singing. Our speaking voices, singing voices, and dispositions improve as soon as we smile. It's a physiological and a psychological process. At the next rehearsal, one of the ladies in the choir presented me with a mirror that all employees in her customer service department kept near their telephones. The mirror reads: "Can your smile be heard?"

Think of three people you would really enjoy visiting today. Do they all have some of the same personal attributes? Are they **nice** to you? Being nice is an obvious trait that is rarely listed on report cards and evaluation forms. But, it is a huge factor in good communications with others.

Do you avoid some people because they are negative toward you? Do they display their negativity by perpetually insulting you? Are you negative toward others by insulting them? What if you discovered a method of building on a person's strengths by offering them a sincere compliment, while avoiding flattery (which is simply telling a lie)? A word of caution: Exercise patience; sometimes it takes a while to find something nice to say about someone. My father very concisely explained his ability to practice patience; he simply said, "I've got the rest of my life." Does the following poem exemplify how negative comments can result in a less than desirable outcome while testing our patience with others? Does this poem remind you of anyone? Hopefully not yourself!

Mothers Poem

He didn't like the casserole
And he didn't like my cake
My biscuits were too hard . . .
Not like his mother used to make.

I didn't perk the coffee right
He didn't like the stew
I didn't mend his socks
The way his mother used to do.

I pondered for an answer
I was looking for a clue.
Then I turned around and smacked him . . .
Just like his Mother used to do!

How many times did the fellow in the poem insult his friend? How often are we guilty of those same types of negative responses toward others? The author of this uniquely crafted poem very skillfully shined the light of **humor** on the situation to indicate the need for change.

I have often said that "humor is the shortest distance between two people." Mark Twain (1835–1910), the American humorist and author, said, "Humor is the great thing, the saving thing. The minute it crops up, all our irritations and resentments slip away and a sunny spirit takes their place." Would you probably agree that it is certainly more appropriate to kindly shine a humorous light on a tense situation than convey unwanted criticism?

Do we always run the risk of our well intentioned humor being misinterpreted? Certainly. That's the chance we take. One day at the conclusion of a class just before lunch, I announced, "Well, I guess I'll go scarf down my peanut butter and jellyfish sandwich." A student very seriously retorted, "I wouldn't do that; I'm a vegetarian!" That student was convinced that I was going to eat jellyfish for lunch. That's the chance ya take . . . oh, well!

HUMOR
Help
Undo
My
Ordinary
Response

A great exercise in effective communications is to list several times you have been complimented recently and several times you have been insulted recently. Think about who gave you the compliments and who insulted you. Does this influence how we select the people we want to associate with? Is this concept becoming very simple?

Now list several times you have complimented someone recently and several times you may have insulted someone. Let's hope you'll have trouble listing anyone you've insulted.

Four Principles of Communication

- We tend to like people who compliment us.
- We tend to like people who display their interest in us.
- We usually attempt to avoid people who insult us.
- We usually attempt to avoid people who fail to be interested in us.

Now you may be thinking, "How do we constructively criticize someone while remaining truthful?" Is effective constructive criticism simply quality instruction? Remember, we have discussed the fact that everyone is a teacher. Is effective teaching simply offering suggestions for change without attacking the personality of the individual? Is there a fine line between constructive criticism and demoralizing personal comments? I recently saw a fellow wearing a shirt that said, "Sarcasm is just one more free service I offer." Was I encouraged to engage him in a conversation? Do you think I would have spoken to him if his shirt would have said, "Let's discover your strengths; we'll build on them; I'm a teacher!"

While I was serving as a school district administrator, I was responsible for (notice I didn't say "in charge of") providing two dozen schools with cultural enrichment assemblies. I worked with the school personnel hosting the performances to facilitate the requirements for ensuring successful presentations. Many of the presenters were provided by the Washington State Arts Commission, of which I was also an advisor. This situation got to be very tricky and a true test for instructive communications.

For openers, I was a member of the committee that advised the state commission on hiring the presenters for the performances. I also helped recruit and develop new presentations to fulfill the needs envisioned by the commission. Then it was my job to select the schools in our district that would host the performances, facilitate the delivery at the performance venue, and evaluate the effectiveness of the project.

Can you imagine the communication challenges involved in this process? Oh, I neglected to mention, this was before the school district was linked with computers. So we communicated the old-fashioned way, by personal visits, group meetings, telephone calls, formal letters, and memos mailed between buildings within our school district and to outside organizations. Talk about advanced planning!

Be very careful in your communications with others and make certain you accurately quote the facts, or your efforts could develop like the following example.

TO: NATIONAL MANAGERS
FROM: CEO, GLOBAL HEADQUARTERS
SUBJECT: HALEY'S COMET

Next Thursday at 10:30, Haley's Comet will spin near the earth. This event occurs only once every 75 years. Notify all the regional managers and have them make arrangements for all employees to assemble on the company lawns and inform them of the occurrence of this phenomenon. If it rains, cancel the outdoors observation and queue up everyone in your auditorium to view a presentation regarding the aging comet.

TO: REGIONAL MANAGERS
FROM: NATIONAL MANAGER
SUBJECT: HALEY'S COMET

By order of Global Headquarters, next Thursday at 10:30 Haley's Comet will spin over the company lawn. Notify all the area managers, an event that occurs every 75 years, that if it rains cancel the remainder of the day's work. Contact Mrs. Barbara Quick to arrange for lunches for everyone and report to the auditorium with all employees where the regional manager will show a phenomenal PowerPoint presentation about our aging company.

TO: AREA MANAGERS
FROM: REGIONAL MANAGER
SUBJECT: HALEY'S COMET

By order of the aging regional manager, at 10:30 next Thursday, Haley's Comet will put a new spin into the PowerPoint presentation. If it rains, ask Barbie Q to serve lunch in the auditorium. If the area manager chickens out, and he's afraid to try just one more PowerPoint presentation, he will join us for lunch, something which occurs only every 75 years.

TO: SITE MANAGERS
FROM: AREA MANAGERS
SUBJECT: HALEY'S COMET

Next Thursday at 10:30, the regional manager will appear in the auditorium with Haley's Comet, rather than take a chance on showing another PowerPoint presentation. If it rains, the aging manager will cancel the comet and BBQ chicken for our lunch, and he will pay the bill, something which occurs only every 75 years.

TO: ALL EMPLOYEES
FROM: SITE MANAGER
SUBJECT: HALEY'S COMET
Because the regional manager has ordered rain for next Thursday at 10:30, we will meet in the auditorium to see a PowerPoint presentation on how to barbeque a phenomenal lunch. Our aging leader will can-

cel all work and appear with some chicks, dancing to the music of Bill Haley . . . and then we'll all get to go for a spin in his '75 Comet.

What are some keys to help avoid saying or writing an incorrect or improper **message** to someone? What are some keys to controlling how we react to messages we receive? Writing letters with paper and pen (does anybody do that any more?) offers different challenges than communicating via electronic methods. While using paper, we have time to contemplate the message, and it is difficult to copy and send to others. Not so with electronic messages! We can crank out e-mail as fast as our fingers can fly and fire it off to people almost anyplace on the planet in a heartbeat. Needless to say, there are a myriad of challenges to effectively using this electronic communication system; consequently it is very easy for people to **spam** others. Technological advances have simply made it way too convenient for us to "shoot, aim, and load!"

MESSAGE
Making
Every
Statement
Significant;
Allowing
Goodness to
Enter

SPAM
Some
People
Are
Mean

Suggestions for Using Electronic Mail

- Know and abide by your organization's policies, rules, and guidelines.
- Imagine you are sending a postcard via regular mail to be read by everyone on the planet.
- After you write the message, allow some time before you send it, especially if you're upset.
- Edit the text while proofreading it from your perspective.

- Proofread the message from the intended recipient's perspective.
- Proofread it from the perspective of whom it might be forwarded to.
- Out of courtesy, reply to important e-mails with at least a "Thanks," "Don't know yet," etc.
- If you reply to an e-mail, consider its impact on everyone it can be forwarded to.
- It is impossible to know the mood of the recipient.
- It is impossible to guarantee the recipient's interpretation of the tone of the message.
- Send only important information and send it only to those who need it; avoid trying to entertain everyone.
- Once you hit the send key it is impossible to recant the message.
- Avoid responding to a negative e-mail; pick up the phone or speak to the person face-to-face.

While writing or making a public presentation, the key to effective communication is to put yourself in the place of the people you are addressing. This task is accomplished by imagining you are the most critical person in the listening or reading audience. This is simply termed playing the devil's advocate.

WTMI
Way
Too
Much
Information

Try to determine the worst thing that someone will say about your message. Then address that issue from their perspective; remember to limit your information to avoid including "Way Too Much Information," commonly referred to as **WTMI.** In the process, try to avoid spilling the beans, selling the farm, muddying the water, or opening a can of worms.

People who blatantly criticize others are called many things: snipers, bullies, tanks, know-it-alls, etc. Remember, we need those kinds of people to help us stay on track. Quite often we shoot the messenger because he or she is simply an easy target. Sure, we know people like to criticize simply because they will be noticed. But remember to always carefully analyze their statements for a possible thread of truth.

Regardless of how hard we work, how we term something, or how passionate we are about the message, we will receive criticism. What do you do when it happens? How do you react? What do you say when people say something that turns your world upside down? Many feel that the most accurate measure of character is how we react to adversity. Is it the problem or how we react to the problem that causes us the most grief? The late Robert Kennedy, while he was secretary of state, summed it up this way: "The cold adverse north winds made the Vikings strong."

Sometimes in an effort to mend a relationship, it's simplest just to admit you're wrong. Swallow your pride, take your lumps, and then try to forget about it. You know that the person tackling the player carrying the football isn't **mad** at the person because they are the ball carrier; the tackler is attacking the ball-carrier's position.

MAD
Meaness
Always
Destroys

Everyone knows this is lot easier said than done. Let's look at an example of how I handled an irate message recipient a few years ago. I had sent a message to the principals in our school district

ANGER
Acclaiming
Negative
Garbage
Eradicates
Relationships

NEEDED
Notice
Everyone's
Esteem
Develop
Each
Day

LUCK
Lanquishing
Using
Current
Knowledge

explaining the procedures for the students from their schools to attend a district-wide music festival. This situation certainly helped me remember Robert Kennedy's statement.

Our district office received a phone call from an extremely angry principal. My, oh my, was he upset! My secretary answered the telephone; she asked if I wished to speak with him. I was thinking about responding that I couldn't talk because my mother was on the phone; however, I reluctantly accepted his call. I knew that it was best to let him vent his **anger** as soon as possible and as long as he **needed.**

The echoes of his yelling at me are probably still reverberating throughout that school district. When he calmed down enough for me to insert a question, I sheepishly asked, "Can I come to your office and hear more about this?" Did I just describe leading a lamb to slaughter?

I was able to determine that he was upset because I had not "officially invited him" to make the decision regarding his music groups' involvement in the festival. We had the festival every year with copious amounts of input from everyone involved. However, he felt that he should have received a formal invitation that allowed him the opportunity to decline the offer for his students to be involved. I hung up the phone and traveled directly to his office. Do you remember what Steve Ballmer of Microsoft said about talking face-to-face? I was wishing that my dentist would call informing me that I needed to have six or seven emergency root canals. No such **luck!**

When I entered the principal's office, he lambasted me for what seemed like an eternity. When he finally started to wind down, I remarked, "I just can't believe that you're this calm. If that message had come to me written that way, I would have been furious. I'm sorry about the words I used in that note; I was extremely presumptuous." After that remark, the wind slithered out of his sails, and we launched into one of the warmest discussions imaginable regarding his hobbies and a mutual friend. Our conversation had evolved into an extremely successful meeting. I was able to heal a festering wound while preserving our future working relationship. What if I leave it to you to decide if his tirade was appropriate in that situation?

Before you say anything about anyone, try taking this test:

- Is what you are saying necessary?
- Is what you are saying kind?
- Is what you are saying true?

Something else to consider before you say something about someone might be this. As you are talking about that person

- Imagine the person is standing right in front of you.
- Imagine their closest friend is standing on their left side.
- Imagine a police officer is standing on their right side.
- Imagine their attorney is standing on your right side.
- Imagine the most critical person you know is standing on your left side.

PRACTICE
Perfecting
Repeated
Actions
Considerably,
To
Increase
Confidence
Everytime

RUMOR
Ridicule
Undermines the
Meaning
Of
Relationships

GOSSIP
Guarded
Old
Secrets
Sensationalized
In
Public

- Imagine a crew is filming all of this to be aired on the six o'clock national news tomorrow night.

Do you remember what our mothers told us? "If you can't say anything nice about a person, don't say anything at all." They were right. We just have to **practice** it. You might consider committing the following statement from the Benevolent Order of the Elks to memory: "Write a person's weaknesses in sand, their strengths in stone!"

Several years ago, I was seated toward the back of a performance hall listening to a vocal jazz contest with three of my choral director friends. We were watching a fellow competitor on stage performing several tunes with his jazz choir for the adjudicators. We spent our time between songs commenting on the percussionist playing in the combo that accompanied the group.

We had plenty of comments to make about the young drummer. We were quite a distance from any of our students, so we weren't concerned about what we were saying. At the conclusion of the group's performance, an elderly couple seated two rows in front of us turned around and remarked, "We couldn't help overhearing what you were saying about the drummer in that last group. We traveled hundreds of miles today to watch him play. Hearing what you said about him was certainly very interesting. We're so thrilled that you think he's so marvelous. We love him too. . . . He's our grandson!" Whew!!!!

Rumors and **gossip** destroy relationships, ruin careers, decimate marriages, drive people insane, escalate into fights, and cause wars. Might rumors and gossip be eliminated from our world if the preceding suggestions were observed? What path do you pursue if an untrue rumor begins to rage out of control?

A few years ago a vicious rumor about me was spreading throughout the school district staff. In an effort to quell that horrible rumor, I asked to have the podium at a district-wide administrators' meeting. Many times, the best route to resolving an issue is the direct route.

I thanked the district staff for deluging me with sincere questions regarding my health. I pointed out that my very slender physique was a product of extreme dieting while running about 250 miles per month training for a marathon. I assured them that, to my knowledge, there had been no announcement at our church to pray for my recovery. To my knowledge, I had not been diagnosed with terminal cancer, and I wasn't planning on dying very soon. However, I sadly reported that two of my friends were battling that dreaded disease. Is it obvious how that gossip began? That brief announcement put a multitude of fallacious rumors about me to rest.

Before you say anything negative about anyone, please remember the **3BS** principle to help keep yourself from being involved in spreading inappropriate rumors. Back Stabbing's Bad Stuff, Be Sincere!

BS
Bad
Stuff,
Back
Stabbing,
Be
Sincere

Sometimes, making an unsolicited comment to a group of individuals can bring unimagined results. Hopefully, it results in good things. A few years ago, our Stadium High School Chanticleer Choir performed at the ribbon-cutting ceremony for the newly refurbished federal courthouse in downtown

Tacoma, Washington. The building previously housed a train station. The beautiful towering rotunda of Union Station possesses magnificent acoustics for enhancing choral sound that I hoped my students could experience in a concert setting.

After the ribbon-cutting ceremony, while I was standing in a circle of people who were unfamiliar to me, I said, "Wouldn't this be a great place to have a holiday choral festival?" Little did I realize that a television producer, Nancy Johnson, was standing in that circle of community leaders.

That simple question led to a series of award-winning television specials entitled "The Gift of Music." Those magnificent specials are still being aired during the holiday season. Hundreds of thousands of viewers continue to enjoy witnessing hundreds of young musicians share their musical gifts. That question provided an additional bonus of many years of friendship with an incredibly intelligent and talented expert in the communications arena.

What if our communications with a person don't proceed the way we had planned? Remember, is it the problem or the way we react to the problem that causes conflict? A few years ago, before we had cell phones (can you imagine life without cell phones), we were shuttling a sick car to a repair shop. Our plan was very simple: My wife was driving to the shop to pick me up after I dropped off our ailing auto. We departed our house after dinner; she was leading the way.

OOPS
Opportunities
Often
Pass
Swiftly

About four miles from home, my ancient car rebelled and succumbed alongside the road . . . as I watched Mary Ann's taillights disappear into the distant darkness. **OOPS!**

Options raced through my mind as I walked about three blocks to a pay phone to call Greg at the repair shop. When Mary Ann arrived at the repair shop, Greg could inform her of my plight, and I'd be saved. Dream on; the repair shop was closed for the night. No big deal; I'll call one of our sons at home. Eeeeerrrrgggghhhh . . . they were both at work. I wasn't going to bother any of my friends. Furthermore, my pride wouldn't allow me to hire a cab. A question struck my mind: "What is the absolute worst thing that can happen in this situation? I'll have to walk home." So what, I needed the exercise anyway.

About an hour later, I arrived at our home to find Mary Ann with a very puzzled look on her face. Had our communications system failed? Could I have blamed her for leaving me stranded? Did we just **laugh** and say "stuff happens?" Did the tow truck company get a phone call? Did I fix **blame** or fix the situation? Did I get some exercise? Did we enjoy our dessert? Chocolate is medicinal!

LAUGH
Levity
Always
Underscores
Good
Habits

BLAME
Big
Losers
Always
Make
Excuses

SUCCESS
Seek Understanding Carefully;
Character Eventually Sows Satisfaction

Throughout this book we have been on a journey to analyze how we might define success in our lives. It is very obvious that everyone possesses a unique combination of interests, desires, and goals. However, there are many common threads entwined in our lives to help us achieve our goals and to ultimately reap satisfaction via those successes.

How do we reach the level of success we are striving for? Hang on, here's the magic word: *try*! When you try and don't like the outcome, just **try** again. The three letters of this word describe the path to success in a very simple, succinct manner. It is comforting to be aware that most of the successful people in the world usually have one profound trait in common. They have all failed more than others simply because they have all tried more than others. Thomas Edison, possibly the greatest inventor who ever lived, illuminated this concept in a very positive fashion by saying, "I have not failed. I've just found 10,000 ways that won't work." Let's explore how this positive approach can help sow satisfaction in our lives.

You will need to search far and wide to find anyone who has failed more at fishing than I have. Do you know why I have been skunked hundreds and hundreds of times? I have failed to catch a fish on hundreds of fishing excursions because I have gone fishing thousands and thousands of times. Do you get the picture? I have failed a lot simply because I

TRY
To
Respect
Yourself

have tried a lot. The expression we use when we fail to catch a fish is "We have been eliminating water." Yes we do need to explore the avenues that are dead ends; we know not to explore them again!

The research for this example has been very easy to complete; I simply glanced at some of the awards in our home. When our son Dave was in his late teens, we decided to form a two-man team and start fishing bass tournaments. Dave procured a twenty-foot Skeeter bass boat powered by a 225-horsepower Yamaha outboard motor. We hopefully assembled all of the necessary equipment to enable us to be competitive in major bass fishing tournaments.

During the summer of 2001, we fished three tournaments without catching a fish. We were doing a fantastic job of exemplifying the definition of the word *failure*! During our fourth tournament, as I was suggesting to Dave that he might have a better chance for success if he found a different partner, a huge bass smashed my lure. I wrestled the four-and-a-half-pound beauty to the boat. We couldn't believe it . . . we actually had a fish to put in our live well. We triumphantly turned on the water pumps to keep the fish healthy so we could present it at the weigh in! Lady luck continued to shine on us that afternoon as we boated three more nice bass to add to the live well. We actually took several fish to the weigh in! We were so proud; even though we didn't win any money, it was our first step that would eventually lead us to success. We fished tournaments the remainder of the season, caught some fish, but failed to win any prize money. We grew accustomed to being debilitated by that deadly dreaded disease diagnosed as failure.

Once that embarrassing season was over, we decided to heed the advice of Bill Belichick, head coach of the world champion New England Patriots football team when he said, "When you live in the past, you'll die in the present." We were looking forward to the future and not just arguing over our disappointing past. During that winter, we began in earnest our mission to improve our chances for success in future tournaments.

Do you remember the marathon story about relating desires to goals? I was able to convince Dave to follow that formula for our needed improvement. We read a plethora of bass fishing materials, watched bass fishing videos, attended fishing seminars, and quizzed many professional bass anglers; we also spent lots of money on high-tech fishing gear. We had dealt with details, done our homework, assembled our equipment by emulating experts; we honed our skills and sharpened our hooks. We felt we were finally thoroughly prepared to be successful in the arena of competitive bass fishing.

We decided to "swing for the fence" and compete with the "big boys" by fishing in the Northwest Bass Tournament Series. The first event of the series was held on Banks Lake in Eastern Washington. I'll never forget the feelings of inferiority that weighed down upon me as eighty-seven big, flashy, high-powered bass boats were launched to compete in the tournament. Looking at the field of competitors was like reciting the list of who's who in the world of competitive bass fishing. I was struggling just to hold down my blueberry pancakes!

Dave and I had a decent day of fishing; however, we didn't expect to place due to the incredible

CONFIDENCE
Changing
Our
Negative
Fears
Invites
Delightful
Experiences
Never
Considered
Easy

BORED
Bring
On
Remembrances
Every
Day

field of highly skilled anglers. At the awards presentation, we could not believe our ears when our
names were announced. We went to the podium
and collected a check for placing sixteenth. We
were absolutely thrilled!

That small taste of success gave us a huge
boost of **confidence** heading into the next tournament on Lake Washington. We decided to invest
hundreds of dollars in an underwater video camera
to help us locate fish in advance of the event. Many
of the other competitors were making use of that
latest legal technology, so we joined the fray. It
was tough for an old guy, but I made a valiant effort
to learn to love technology! I spent hours and hours
scouring the watery depths of Lake Washington
with the camera. It was fun for a while, but then I
became really **bored**. However, during the search, I
located several schools of nice-sized smallmouth
bass we hoped would be hungry for our lures on the
day of the tournament. We were pumped!

Tournament day arrived with rainy, blustery
conditions churning the lake's surface into a froth.
We lucked out in the draw for starting position and
blasted off in the seventh slot to race to our favorite
spot. Away we flew, at seventy miles per hour,
crashing from wave to wave with the heavy rain
pelting our faces while our cheeks were being
blown back to our ears. Gee, that ride was fun . . .
when it was over! We got to the spot we had hoped
for. Dave nailed a nice fish on his third cast . . . such
a great way to begin! We rotated through four
spots as the day unfolded; we caught lots and lots
of fish. We began discussing the possibility of actually winning first place in the tournament. We

were shaking with anticipation of the possibility of great things to come at the awards presentation.

The weigh-in ceremony was an event that **dreams** are made of. The two-person teams weighed in their five largest bass of the day. There was also a cash prize for the single biggest bass. I had landed two big ones: both over five pounds. The moment of **truth** approached as our fish were placed on the scale; my heart was pounding so loud I was afraid I wouldn't be able to hear the announcement. We were in the lead by less than one ounce . . . eeeeeooow!

The remainder of the teams weighed in, and nobody else came close to our weight. We won the award for big fish of the tournament, plus we collected several thousand dollars in first place prize money. At long last, success had shined down upon our fishing team!

As the season progressed, a different team of anglers won each of the first five events of the tournament series. The sixth and final competition was held at a site unfamiliar to us, Crow Butte State Park on the Columbia River. So before the tournament, I traveled there to familiarize myself with the waters and hopefully determine how to catch a prize-winning bag of bass.

Dinks. I caught dinks, dinks, dinks. Lots and lots and lots of dinks. The water was deluged with those little dinks! You have to catch three- and four-pounders to have a chance of doing well in a tournament at this high level of competition. The biggest fish I caught were only about two pounds—dinks!

The Columbia River is a huge body of water; we needed lots of information to have any hope of

DREAMS
Desire
Reflects
Eventual
Achievements
Magically
Secured

TRUTH
To
Rely
Upon
Their
Honor

being successful. Fortunately, I was able to chat with several local fishermen regarding their successful methods of catching fish in that area. A kind professional bass guide from Kennewick, Washington, Bob Adkinson was very generous in providing me with his detailed methods of success. He told me which lures to use, how to present them, and some specific spots to fish.

Because of our lack of experience fishing that area, the steep entry fee, and the high price of fuel, Dave and I discussed the possibility of not competing in that tournament. I finally said, "Look, Dave, if we win that tournament, we would be the only team to win two of the six events. Let's give it a try." After a lengthy discussion, he very reluctantly agreed that we should at least try. So we began our long journey to the tournament site.

The time arrived for blastoff, the sun was peeping over the rolling hills, the water was like a sheet of glass; it was a picture perfect, beautiful warm August morning. We raced many miles to a spot I had selected by studying a map of the contour of the points on the river. When we stopped at our predetermined spot, we were greeted by a bevy of bass busting on the water's surface as they chased bait fish for breakfast. Talk about **fun**: They were biting on everything we threw at them. It was a sensational morning of fishing! We rapidly filled our live well with a limit of nice smallmouth bass we hoped might put us in the prize money. It was hard to believe that we were experiencing so much success in a tournament that we had no **confidence** in entering.

As the day progressed, the wind began blowing and increased in intensity until it was howling. We

FUN
Forget
Unnecessary
Nonsense

CONFIDENCE
Changing
Our
Negative
Fears
Invites
Delightful
Experiences
Never
Considered
Easy

decided to proceed carefully back to the launch area, hoping to find larger fish on the way. Unfortunately, as time went by, the fish seemed to develop lockjaw; we hadn't had a strike in hours.

Late in the afternoon, we motored into the bay where the boat launch was located. With about thirty minutes remaining until our official weigh-in time, we decided to try our **luck** just across the small bay from the boat ramp even though we knew that most of the other fisherman in the tournament had already fished that shoreline. The wind was gusting to about 35 miles per hour; the trolling-motor batteries were all but dead; and waves were crashing into the boat—not a pleasant experience. At that point we were just hoping to stay afloat!

As you might imagine, those conditions precipitated the most intense argument our fishing team had ever experienced. As we were drifting along the rocky shoreline casting our lures into the pounding surf, Dave screamed, "Dad, this is the stupidest thing we've ever done; we don't have enough big fish to win any money. You know that we haven't had a bite in hours; let's just put the boat on the trailer and go home." I yelled back, "Dave, keep trying; if we can nail just one big fish, we can win this tournament and be the only team to win two." He was becoming extremely agitated; he started screaming about my insistence on trying to catch "Moby Dick" during the "Perfect Storm."

While he continued screaming at me, I was trying to think of how to avoid being involved in our first ever knock-down, drag-out fistfight. Suddenly, I realized that his screams were taking on a different tone. He was screaming about an entirely new topic. He

LUCK
Lanquishing
Using
Current
Knowledge

was bellowing, "Fish! ... fish! ... fish! ... fish!" We couldn't believe our eyes! The largest bass we had ever seen was hurling herself into the air attempting to throw Dave's hooks. Miraculously, in spite of the howling wind, the crashing waves, and the dead trolling-motor batteries, we were able to wrestle the behemoth bass on board.

Guess who won that tournament? Guess who collected thousands of dollars in prize money? Guess who has become a Skeeter Bass Boat Pro Staffer, sponsored by Outboard Center in Arcata, California? The monster largemouth bass tipped the scale at over nine pounds. At that time, it was the largest bass ever recorded in a tournament in the state of Washington. Throughout the yearlong tournament series we had experienced a firsthand lesson that unequivocally paved our path to success: Don't look back, do your homework, seek advice, get organized, believe in yourself, be patient, be tolerant, and work hard. And most importantly, just keep trying!

Let's look at an example to analyze how success may be much more than winning a material prize. Early in my career a life-changing event took place when I flew to Prestwick, Scotland, as the conductor of a choir comprised of students from several Northwest states. My school choirs had been amassing awards at home, and I wanted to continue the string of smashing successes in Europe with the members of the Northwest Folksingers. The members of our summer choir had rehearsed on weekends throughout the winter and spring perfecting a wide array of American music to share on our six-week European tour. We sang in many magnificent venues: Tivoli Garden Concert Hall, Kaiser Wilhelm Church, Berlin Philharmonic Hall, and others. Many of the performances were at festivals involving choirs from throughout the world. Our goal in each performance was to be the best choir there, absolutely no questions asked!

Our first major performance took place in Scotland at an outdoor festival held on a magnificent rolling lawn in front of an ancient castle overlooking a lake. Many terrific choirs were being featured at the festival. The Northwest Folksingers were scheduled to sing second to last, a great spot in the performance order to enable us to blow 'em away. Even though the event was not organized as a competition, the fire was burnin' in my belly to be the best. When it was our turn to perform, we absolutely electrified the crowd. At the conclusion of our set of songs, the audience leapt to their feet and gave us the greatest ovation of the evening. We had won . . . at least in our eyes.

As you might imagine, my ego was once again thoroughly deluged with a concoction of arrogance and pride. After our earth-shaking performance, I wasn't at all concerned about any competition from the choir of seasoned singers who were waiting for their turn on stage. After our spell-binding performance, the Glasgow-Phoenix Choir methodically assembled on the risers.

The faces of the choir members immediately lit up when Peter Mooney began conducting. They seemed to be so thrilled and happy to be sharing their magnificent music. Reminiscent of my seventh-grade experience of hearing John play his trumpet, once again my jaw started toward the earth. Once again, fortunate for my face, the ground still wasn't too far away.

The Glasgow-Phoenix Choir had such a beautiful tone; they sounded as though they were in love with singing, in love with themselves, in love with one another, and in love with their director. How dare they share those intimate feelings by singing so expressively? I was flabbergasted! When they started singing their final song, I lapsed into a total meltdown. I cried and cried and cried while they so beautifully shared their love of one another and of their homeland by singing the Scottish folk song "Loch Lomond" as we were on the hill overlooking . . . Loch Lomond!

Did my concept of success change because of that experience? Is success simply winning a sporting event or a trophy, receiving acclaim or money? Or is true success the quality of our character measured by the depth of love in our relationships—the primary relationship with the person currently wearing our clothes and how that relationship resonates with others?

Norman Vincent Peale (1898–1993), the author of the "Power of Positive Thinking", had these words by Stephen Grellet (1773–1855), a Quaker Missionary, attached to his bathroom mirror so he could read them daily:

> I expect to pass through this world but once. Any good thing, therefore, that I can do or any kindness that I can show to a fellow creature . . . let me do it now. Let me not defer or neglect it, for I shall not pass this way again.

Mother Teresa had this wish for people of the world:

> Be happy in the moment; that's enough. Each moment is all we need, not more. Be happy now and, if you show through your actions that you love others, including those who are poorer than you, you'll give them happiness, too. It doesn't take much—it can be just giving a smile. The world would be a much better place if everyone smiled more. So smile; be cheerful; be joyous . . .

Bill and Melinda Gates were recently featured on a local television newscast. Their appearance was a definite attention grabber considering that we are accustomed to seeing Mr. Gates in a totally different light. His television appearances have usually been in connection with the latest and greatest software innovations from Microsoft.

This newscast chronicled how the Bill and Melinda Gates Foundation contributes more than one billion dollars per year fighting poverty in the developing countries of the world. It was certainly a stark contrast to view the world's wealthiest man and woman sharing their love as they were strolling among the poorest of the poor in a far-off land.

Mr. and Mrs. Gates seemed to be so much in **love** with what they were doing and in love with one another. They seemed to be so at **peace** and so incredibly **happy** about leaving their **legacy**. Even though I have oftentimes marveled at their magnificent home gracing the shores of Lake

LOVE
Light's
On
Very
Empowering

PEACE
Practicing
Effective
Attitudes
Calms
Everyone

HAPPY
Have
All the
Peace 'n
Pleasure
Ya want

LEGACY
Let
Every
Gift
Attribute
Compliments to
You

HOME
Happiness
Only
Means
Everything

LIFE
Love
Is
For
Everyone

WEALTH
Wishing
Everyone
Achieves
Love'n
Total
Happiness

Washington, it seemed as though they had truly discovered a new **home**.

As I was analyzing the aura that seemed to be enveloping Bill and Melinda, I was struck with the realization of what **life** might really be about. Should our level of success be measured by the amount of financial wealth that we accumulate during our lifetimes? Or should the measure of our success simply be a matter of how we ultimately interpret the implications of the word *wealth*?

Wishing

Everyone

Achieves

Love 'n'

Total

Happiness

About the Author

Bruce Brummond has helped thousands develop their SELF-WORTH (Securing Esteem Lessens Fear, Working Offers Respect Triggering Happiness) while maximizing their potential to achieve SUCCESS (Seek Understanding Carefully, Character Eventually Sows Satisfaction). He has shared his talents as a salesman, commercial fisherman, competitive bass fisherman, music educator, school district administrator, and motivational speaker.

Bruce is the owner and founder of Character Construction Company, an organization dedicated to assisting individuals and organizations enhance their INTEGRITY (Individuals Never Trust Evil, Golden Rule Inspires Their Years) while reaching their GOALS (Greatness Only Awaits Labor... Start!).

Appendix

Ordering Information

You can order
The Book. . .

1. **"Acronyms Building Character, the ABC's of Life"**

The poster of Skipper that says. . .

2. **"SOUL—Source Of Unconditional Love"**

at www.atlasbooks.com
or by calling 1-800BOOKLOG

༄

To schedule a seminar or event
with Bruce Brummond, contact him at
http://www.characterconstructioncompany.com